GROWING CHRYSANTHEMUMS

GROWING CHRYSANTHEMUMS

Harry Randall
and
Alan Wren

CHRISTOPHER HELM London
TIMBER PRESS Portland, Oregon

Christopher Helm (Publishers) Ltd,
Imperial House,
21-25 North Street,
Bromley, Kent BR1 1SD

Reprinted 1985
First published in paperback 1987

British Library Cataloguing in Publication Data

Randall, Harry
Growing Chrysanthemums.
1. Chrysanthemums
I. Title II. Wren, Alan
635.9′3355 SB413.C55

ISBN 0-7470-2804-4

First published in the USA in 1983 by
Timber Press,
9999 SW Wilshire,
Portland,
OR 97225, USA

ISBN 0-88192-041-X

Printed and bound in Great Britain by
Biddles Ltd, Guildford and King's Lynn

Contents

List of Figures	vii
Acknowledgements	ix
Foreword	xi
Introduction	13
1. The Real Beginning	18
2. Wintering Stools and Buying Plants	27
3. Propagation	37
4. Composts and Soils	46
5. Potting Up and Hardening	60
6. Potting On Into Second Pots	65
7. Stopping and Timing	68
8. Planting the Earlies	78
9. Final Pots for Lates	81
10. The Growing Season	86
11. Flowering the Earlies	104
12. Flowering Lates	111
13. Exhibition	117
14. Cut Blooms for Home Decoration	127
15. Special Treatments	129
16. Troubles – and Cures	135
17. A Calendar Guide	138
18. A Deeper Insight	146
Appendix I: Conversion Table	162
Appendix II: Society Addresses	163
Index	166

List of Figures

2.1	Earlies Stools Trimmed and Sterilised Ready for Boxing	30
2.2	Tray of Stools Carrying a Crop of Cuttings	30
3.1	Three Prepared Cuttings – the Centre Cutting is Close to the Ideal	37
3.2	Cuttings Inserted in the Bed on the Greenhouse Staging	40
3.3	Inserting a Cutting in the Bed	42
3.4	Rooted Cuttings – Ready for Potting, Boxing or Bedding	44
3.5	Cuttings to be Rooted – Five to a Three-inch Pot	44
3.6	Cuttings Rooted in a Tray	45
5.1	A Well-established Plant in its First Pot	61
5.2	Frame Ventilation by Means of Stepped Wedges	63
6.1	A Strong Root System Ready for Potting on into a Larger Pot	66
7.1	Natural Development of a Chrysanthemum	69
7.2	Plant not yet in Stopping Condition	72
7.3	Plant in Stopping Condition	73
7.4	The Two-leaf Stop	73
7.5	The "Run-by"	77
8.1	Planting out an Early	79
9.1	Final Potting	83
10.1	Lateral in Need of Disbudding and Deshooting and Lateral Disbudded and Deshooted	88
10.2	Plant Carrying Four Laterals	89
10.3	Four-lateral Disbudded Plant Staked Ready for Flowering	89
10.4	"Long-V" Lateral	91
10.5	Shoot Tip before Deshooting and Disbudding	96
10.6	Bud Swelling after Deshooting and Disbudding	96
10.7	Growing Tip becomes Flower Bud	97
10.8	Bud Initiation to Colour Show	97
10.9	Cell Division and Vacuolation	98
11.1	Blooms in Polythene Bags	104
11.2	A Simple Overhead Cover for Protecting Earlies	106
11.3	Bud Ready for Protection	106
11.4	Bags over Buds of Earlies	107

11.5 A Floret is Composed of Millions of Cells 108
13.1 An Unprepared Reflex 122
13.2 The Same Bloom Tidied at the Crown for Exhibition 122
13.3 Incurves – the Bloom on the Left is Loose and Untidy at the Base 124
18.1 Lateral Cross-section of Floret 151
18.2 A Floret Changing from Incurving to Reflexing 158

Acknowledgements

While the preparation of this book may have been a personal activity, many good friends in the chrysanthemum world in a number of countries have contributed to its content, in that they have played their part in the fullness of our experience and understanding of our mutual subject. We value such friendships, exchanges and occasional associations. More specifically, we owe much to the tolerance of our wives, Eva and Sheila, and we must pay further tribute to Eva for spending so many hours at the typewriter unravelling almost unreadable copy. Our sincere thanks go to our good friends Barrie Machin, for vetting the end product, and Joe Millett of California and Carl Wallace for their assistance with colour and black and white photographs.

Foreword

It gives me great pleasure to write this foreword because both Harry Randall and Alan Wren have been my good friends and colleagues for many years through our mutual love of chrysanthemums.

In this book they have put together in a very readable form all the essential ingredients of knowledge required to grow quality chrysanthemums. No detail of culture has been overlooked, yet at the same time many new and interesting facts regarding the growth and development of chrysanthemum plants through the season are discussed relative to growing practices.

A careful study of this book by even an experienced grower will give him much to think about and will certainly increase his knowledge and therefore equip him more fully to reach the very highest levels in chrysanthemum growing.

The newcomer to growing chrysanthemums will find the book a veritable mine of essential information. The detailed description of each cultivation technique leaves no unanswered questions for the beginner and I would thoroughly recommend that the advice given is followed to the letter.

I would particularly highlight the emphasis laid on the necessity for understanding the optimum conditions for healthy root growth. This is essential for the maintenance of the correct nutrition of the plant at each phase of its life cycle. The authors have left no stone unturned in this very important area of consideration.

I particularly enjoyed and learnt much from their tips on the preparation of blooms for exhibition and on all the other details, apart from cultural ones, which need to be considered by the successful exhibitor.

The book is very well illustrated and the excellent line drawings relating to the various aspects of husbandry as the plant develops are perfectly complementary to the text.

I have no hesitation in recommending this book to all who grow or wish to grow chrysanthemums of all types to the best possible standards.

Dr Barrie Machin,
Felpham, Sussex.

Introduction

The chrysanthemum is unique among horticultural subjects. No other species appears in such a wide range of plant types, bloom forms and colours. Bonsai chrysanthemums can be produced as tiny flowering "trees" no more than a foot in height; charms grow as deep mushroom-shaped plants up to 3 ft in diameter, covered in small, scented, single flowers; cascades, as befits their name, are grown into long pendulous drapes of blooms – they can also be trained as large fans or pillars; huge specimen plants can reach up to 12-15 ft in circumference with a hundred or more disbudded blooms.

We can enjoy blooms single in form, delicate spiders, quills, spoons and conventional double-flowered incurves, intermediates and reflexes. Colours range from white and cream, through every shade of yellow, pink, bronze and red to deep purple – and even green. Blooms vary in size from half an inch in the case of bonsai, through small-flowered pompons and sprays to the massive 10 in blooms of the large exhibition range.

It is hardly surprising that in addition to its unparalleled use for commercial purposes the chrysanthemum is widely grown by amateurs, many of whom specialise in one or more of the various types, in particular those producing specimen blooms by disbudding techniques.

Spray chrysanthemums can be grown for garden and home decoration with little attention through the growing season, but greater rewards are to be had for extra care and attention. In fact, the chrysanthemum is a responsive subject. It may let us down if we neglect it, but it repays dedicated and skilled cultivation with plants and blooms which enjoy an exalted position in the eyes of keen horticulturists.

Members of the chrysanthemum family are to be found as natives of many countries all over the world, but the chrysanthemum so greatly revered by the specialist grower and produced in vast numbers commercially have emerged from *Chrysanthemum indicum* and *Chrysanthemum sinense*, natives of China and Japan.

The Chinese were undoubtedly among the first to cultivate the chrysanthemum. Confucius recorded the fact in 500BC, and it seems probable that it was cultivated long before this, though the types then available are thought to have been limited to small yellow and mauve-pink singles.

Although both *Chrysanthemum indicum* and *Chrysanthemum sinense* grow wild in Japan, the Japanese are said to have imported the cultivated Chinese varieties and to have used them as the basis of their own important hybridising developments, cross-fertilising the imported varieties with other wild Japanese types. Inevitably, details of such early activities are vague, and reports are in conflict. One suggestion is that Chinese varieties reached Japan via Korea in 386 AD; another claims that it was not until the eighth century. What seems certain, however, is that it was the Chinese who conducted the early pioneer work on the species, that the Japanese subsequently made dramatic advances, and that these improved cultivated varieties remained as a highly esteemed prerogative of the gardeners of the Orient for many centuries before finding their way to Europe and across the world.

The Chinese saw fit to name a city, Chu-hsien (Chrysanthemum City), in honour of the flower; the Japanese were equally indulgent, instituting a Chrysanthemum Day, or Festival of Happiness, adopting a single-flowered chrysanthemum as the crest and official seal of the Emperor, and making the Imperial Order of the Chrysanthemum the highest order of chivalry in the land.

Holland appears to have been the first European country to have imported chrysanthemums from the East, in 1688 – but they did not survive. Then in 1789 M. Blancard, of Marseilles, imported three varieties into France from China, one of which, "Old Purple", survived to take its place in chrysanthemum history. It was probably this variety which was grown in England in 1795, and which was referred to as "a handsome chrysanthemum". A few years later a hundred new varieties are said to have reached Paris.

Eight varieties arrived in England from China in the late eighteenth and early nineteenth centuries, and 24 were in existence in 1824, with the number increasing to 48 (though one report says 60) by 1826. Further expeditions were sent to China and Japan in the mid-nineteenth century. Robert Fortune's journey to Japan from England in 1860 was to prove of considerable significance, for the varieties he procured had "great size", completely new flower forms and a greater range of colours – proof of the skill of the Japanese hybridists. Fortune acquired some 30 new varieties, and although only 12 or 15 are said to have survived to reach England they provided our hybridists with exciting new material. Hybridists were also at work elsewhere, notably in France and the Channel Islands, and it was undoubtedly this period of chrysanthemum development which laid the foundations of its universal popularity.

Chrysanthemum cultivation was said to have been "taken up with feverish excitement by our cousins on the other side of the Atlantic" in the late nineteenth century, and chrysanthemums are said to have reached Tasmania from England in 1836, and to have been grown in New South Wales, Australia, in 1843. They were "well established" in Victoria in 1855. It was New Zealand's turn in the 1860s. Many other countries could be added to the list. The chrysanthemum has indeed become an international flower, with considerable globular exchange in types and varieties, in cultural techniques, and not least in personal friendships.

Such a widely grown subject is required to perform satisfactorily under differing climatic conditions, and some types are better suited to particular regions than others. Brightly coloured large-flowered disbuds are not at their best in warm climates, and consequently where temperatures are high the smaller-flowered types have become more popular. Similarly, fashions vary.

In Britain, the north-western states of the USA and in Canada disbudded specimen blooms are predominant, and the same could be said for Australia and New Zealand. But in other parts of the USA the delicate spiders, quills and spoons are widely grown, and these latter types are becoming more universally popular. Oriental growers, on the other hand, excel in the training of plants into artistic forms.

One might well ask, therefore, how the cultivation of so many types of chrysanthemum under widely differing conditions can be covered in one volume. The answer is that the requirements of all chrysanthemums, their pattern of development and their cultural needs, are fundamentally the same. In the following chapters we shall be looking into the important principles of each phase of development, and we shall be presenting a basic pattern of cultivation step by step through the season which can be used for all types of chrysanthemum, but which can be modified according to individual circumstances and varying climatic conditions. But while basic cultural requirements are similar, a number of specialist types call for somewhat different management, and we have added a chapter to cover their needs in more detail.

Growing plants have specific requirements, and if cultivation is to be calculated as opposed to casual we must appreciate their needs and provide for them. With this in mind we shall be looking lightly into some of the fascinating inner functions of the plant insofar as such insight is likely to lead to better and more consistent results. An intimate knowledge of plant functions is by no means essential to chrysanthemum success. Many prominent growers know little of such matters, and at the other extreme students of plant biology can make poor plantsmen. But a measure of understanding of the workings of the plant is obviously desirable and must intensify interest and involvement. How deeply one delves is a personal decision. There are those whose needs are met by a simple but sound general coverage, but there are always others who desire to probe more deeply. We have endeavoured to cater for both.

We have also prepared a chapter presenting the season's cultural routine in condensed calendar form, which can be used as a reference week by week through the year. Our calendar is based on the timing of activities in Britain; it will need modification in respect of dates by growers in other countries. Growers in the Southern Hemisphere will need to adjust British dates by a period of six months – our January activities become July and so on. Other personal variations may be desirable, but the essential principles and cultural notes provide for the basic needs of the plant and will be valid under all circumstances and climates.

Though we have both exhibited extensively – and successfully – we look upon exhibiting as desirable but by no means vital. In our view the first consideration is the enjoyment of the season's round of cultivation, taking day-to-day satisfaction from the progress of one's plants, and finally the enjoyment of beautiful blooms. But exhibiting is a wonderful extra indulgence which is bound to lead to improved results, and firm personal friendships are sure to emerge. Shows are indeed an important stimulus to the chrysanthemum movement, and we have therefore given advice on exhibiting and the presentation of blooms.

We have not listed and given separate cultural advice on popular present-day varieties for the various sections. With such a wide-ranging subject this would have taken up many pages, and in many cases varieties are superseded relatively quickly. Rather, we have made use of the available space to present a detailed and reasonably comprehensive cultural routine which will stand the test of time. Details of varieties can be readily obtained from nurserymen's catalogues.

Visits to shows and to other growers will also give guidance concerning the best varieties to grow and comparisons will do much to sharpen further one's own cultural skills. In fact the real fullness of chrysanthemum activities can only be savoured as a result of association and involvement with others of similar outlook. Fortunately, there are many specialist chrysanthemum societies serving the needs of growers, and membership can lead to constant interesting exchanges. In addition, the National Chrysanthemum Society supplies a steady flow of topical literature to its members, and regional groups cover the interests of their members on an area basis. Other bodies and facilities are in existence in other countries. Brief details are provided in the Appendix.

We have looked at the main pests and diseases as they occur through the season rather than prepare a stereotyped chapter with information on problems seldom, if ever, encountered.

Our final chapter is designed to cater in particular for those of a progressive outlook, delving a little more deeply into certain aspects of bloom quality and perchance opening the door to future profitable personal deductions.

CHAPTER 1

The Real Beginning

What To Grow

One of the first decisions must be what to grow, and with such a wide range of plant types and bloom forms this can be difficult. The choice will depend on circumstances and personal outlook.

Varieties available to the public are classified by specialist bodies according to plant type, bloom type, bloom colour, bloom size and season of flowering, and in reference lists and catalogues the names of varieties are followed by simple code numbers and letters to indicate these characteristics. In Britain the National Chrysanthemum Society is responsible for the classification of chrysanthemums, and the system it operates can provide the newcomer with a clear insight into the available range.

The system consists of thirty sections: Sections 1 to 12 covering late-flowering varieties for flowering in a greenhouse (usually in November); Sections 13 to 19 October-flowering; and Sections 23 to 30 early-flowering varieties which will flower in the open garden by the end of September.

Late-flowering

Section 1 – Large Exhibition

Large blooms up to 10 in or more in diameter, in various bloom forms. Looked upon by many as the ultimate test of the grower's skill. Usually grown at one bloom to the plant.

Section 2 – Medium Exhibition

Large blooms, but smaller than Large Exhibition. Usually 7 in, 8 in or a little more in diameter. Various bloom forms. Grown at one or two blooms to the plant.

Section 3 – Incurved

Spherical blooms with florets (petals) incurving toward the crown. Perfection when well grown. Blooms normally 4 in to 5 in in diameter. Usually grown at two or three blooms to the plant. This section is sub-divided into (a) large-flowered, (b) medium-flowered, (c) small-flowered.

Section 4 – Reflexed

Blooms in this section have florets which turn over into reflexing form; 4 in to 6 in in diameter. Sleek reflexes are indeed attractive. Usually two or three blooms to the plant. Sub-divided into (a) large-flowered, (b) medium-flowered, (c) small-flowered.

Section 5 – Intermediate

Blooms are 4 in to 6 in in diameter, with either closely or loosely incurving florets, frequently showing both sides of the floret to pleasing effect. Two or three blooms to the plant. Sub-divided into (a) large-flowered, (b) medium-flowered, (c) small-flowered.

Section 6 – Anemones

Anemones are different, in that they are single in form, with a prominent domed central cushion of small disc florets. At best very attractive, but with all too few representatives. Generally 4 in to 5 in in diameter. Grown at four to six blooms per plant. Sub-divided into (a) large-flowered, (b) medium-flowered, (c) small-flowered.

Section 7 – Singles

As their title suggests, blooms in this section have only a few rows of "petals" with a central "disc" of disc florets. Blooms from 3 in to 6 in or more in diameter. Grown at four to six per plant for large-flowered varieties, and up to ten or twelve for medium and small. Sub-divided into (a) large-flowered, (b) medium-flowered, (c) small-flowered.

Section 8 – Pompons

Small ball-shaped blooms, with tiny florets. Can be grown up to 2 in in diameter when disbudded to one bloom per stem. Unfortunately a somewhat neglected type. Can be cropped at ten to twelve disbudded blooms to the plant or grown and exhibited as sprays. Sub-divided into (a) true poms (globular in form), (b) semi-poms (flat based and more mushroom shaped).

Section 9 – Sprays

An increasingly popular subject available in a range of bloom forms. The very best sprays can carry 20 or more blooms on the stem. Sub-divided into (a) anemones, (b) pompons, (c) reflexed, (d) singles, (e) intermediate, (f) spiders, quills, spoons and any other types.

Section 10 – Spiders, Quills, Spoons

At best, three beautiful types. Spiders can be grown to 8 in or more in diameter, with long tubular florets curled at the tips and generally falling over from the central button into reflexing form. Quills have similar quilled florets, but they are straight to the tip, and consequently blooms are more spiky in character. Spoons are single in form with very attractive florets, which are tubular for most of their length but opening out and flattening at the tip to give a spoonlike appearance. Sub-divided into (a) spiders, (b) quills, (c) spoons.

Section 11 – Any other types

A virtual safety valve in the classification system to cater for any type which does not fall into the other sections, and seldom used.

Section 12 – Charms and Cascades

Charms are plants which grow as dense small-leaved domes covered in small, scented flowers so closely grouped as to completely clothe the circumference. A well-grown charm will be 2 ft or more in diameter. Every chrysanthemum grower should have a few in his collection.

Cascades are trained down canes to form pendulous plants a foot or more across and 3 ft to 5 ft in length. A somewhat demanding, but magnificent, subject.

October-flowering

Section 13 – Incurved

As Section 3, but can be flowered in the open garden in frost-free localities. Subdivided into (a), (b) and (c).

Section 14 – Reflexed

Details as Section 4.

Section 15 – Intermediate

Details as Section 5.

Section 16 – Large October-flowering

Created as a section to cater for large-flowered varieties introduced some years ago, but now seldom seen.

Section 17 – Singles

Details as Section 7.

Section 18 – Pompons

Details as Section 8.

Section 19 – Sprays

Details as Section 9.

Section 20 – Any other types.

Early-flowering

Section 23 – Incurved

Details as Section 3, but with fewer representatives.

Section 24 – Reflexed

As Section 4, but with a wide coverage of varieties in all sizes and colours. A very popular section.

Section 25 – Intermediate

As Section 5. Again a very popular section, with many quality representatives.

Section 26 – Anemones

As Section 6, but few representatives in the early range and only sub-sections (a) large-flowered, (b) medium-flowered.

Section 27 – Singles

As Section 7, but again poorly represented and seldom seen. Sub-sections (a) large-flowered, (b) medium-flowered.

Section 28 – Pompons

As Section 8 and only a few popular varieties.

Section 29 – Sprays

As Section 9 and a great many quality varieties now available. Less demanding than disbuds; can be flowered without protection. Deservedly popular for home and garden decoration and for exhibition.

Section 30 – Any other types.

Few horticultural species can boast such a range of colours as the chrysanthemum, and it is obviously desirable that lists of varieties and catalogues should be able to indicate bloom colour clearly. The British National Chrysanthemum Society has covered the need by listing 21 different colour groupings, and each new variety is placed in one of these groups at the time of its classification. The colours are indicated by their initials, which, together with section and size codings, then follow the name of the variety. The groupings are as follows:

W	White	LB	Light Bronze
C	Cream	B	Bronze
LY	Light Yellow	DB	Deep Bronze
Y	Yellow	LR	Light Red
DY	Deep Yellow	R	Red
LP	Light Pink	DR	Deep Red
P	Pink	LPu	Light Purple
DP	Deep Pink	Pu	Purple
LS	Light Salmon	DPu	Deep Purple
S	Salmon	O	Other Colours (Green, etc.)
DS	Deep Salmon		

Thus, a large-flowered, late-flowering incurve, yellow in colour, would be classified 3aY; a medium-flowered, late-flowering single, deep red in colour, would be classified 7bDR; and an outdoor early-flowering reflex, small-flowered and light pink in colour, would be 24cLP.

Bonsai, though in limited circulation in the UK, are not included in the classification system at present, but for the artistically minded they can be very rewarding if stock can be found.

Other countries have somewhat different classifications, but they are similar in principle, in that they channel the various varieties into a set of groupings.

In all classification systems most of the sections are for disbudded specimen blooms, and the great majority of specialist growers concentrate mainly on these types. We shall therefore centre our cultural pattern on disbudded types, with passing reference to other sections, in the belief that by so doing we shall be looking into the needs and workings of the plant in considerable detail. We shall be covering cultivation as demanded by the variable British climate, which will make for consideration of the effects of cold and heat, wind and rain. In so doing we shall be providing the most comprehensive coverage.

In Britain, early-flowering varieties are flowered in the open, though frequently with some form of protection against wind and rain, and October-flowering varieties can in many cases be cultivated in the same way, but late-flowering types, though grown in pots in the open in the summer months, need accommodating in a greenhouse for flowering. Whether or not a greenhouse is available can therefore influence the decision on what to grow. In warmer countries greenhouses may not be necessary.

How Many To Grow

Having decided what to grow, the next important consideration is how many plants can be conveniently managed. Again this is a very personal decision. There are plenty of growers who derive great pleasure from just a few dozen plants, but the enthusiast is more likely to be handling in the region of fifty to a hundred earlies or up to fifty lates, and the really keen showman may have several hundred earlies or up to two hundred or more lates. The newcomer would be well advised to begin with a reasonably small collection and build up over the space of a few years. Whatever the decisions, the aim should be quite clear: to produce quality blooms and enjoy the activity. The numbers grown should never be so great as to make this impossible.

Which Varieties

The next decision, and equally important, is which varieties to choose. Catalogue descriptions tend to paint everything in glowing colours, but there are other pointers which should be heeded. The National Chrysanthemum Society operates an award system which gives valuable guidance on the merit of varieties. There are three main awards: the PC (Preliminary Commendation) for exhibition or for cut-flower purposes, the only award open to a variety when it is first placed before the classification committee; the AM (Award of Merit), given only to established varieties of proven merit; and the

FCC (First Class Certificate), awarded to varieties of outstanding merit. Varieties with the coveted FCC must certainly be considered, followed by those with an AM, and new varieties with a PC will warrant watching in the future. Another valuable pointer at shows is the popularity of varieties – those which appear frequently and win frequently can be looked upon as being consistent and relatively easy to grow, as well as being meritorious. If in doubt seek advice from experienced growers and nurserymen suppliers.

Stock Selection Is Important

Not everyone who reads these pages will be a virtual newcomer to chrysanthemums. Many will be established growers at varying levels of proficiency. The newcomer's season will commence with the purchase of plants, but the established grower's will begin with the selection of stock from last year's plants, and it is from this point that we shall begin to work through the season, starting with stock selection and progressing phase by phase to bloom maturity.

Varietal characteristics are not retained in chrysanthemums raised from seed, and the various varieties are therefore propagated by means of cuttings from last year's stools. The cuttings should always be taken from those stools which have produced the finest flowers.

Unfortunately, we can be faced with other problems which make selection even more important, namely debilitating diseases and pests which can be passed on through successive generations of cuttings. For example, more than 20 different viruses have been found in chrysanthemums, some affecting bloom quality, some affecting foliage, and each automatically transmitted to next season's cuttings with any debilitating effects.

Tomato Aspermy Virus reduces bloom size, distorts florets and leads to colour loss and streaking in other than whites and yellows. Once Aspermy Virus becomes firmly established in a plant the effects are severe and obvious, and they occur in all the blooms on the plant. But there are no foliar symptoms. The effects of some other viruses, while also reducing bloom quality, are less obvious, and therefore vigilant selection while plants are in flower should become an automatic part of the cultural routine.

In other cases the symptoms are vegetative, again in some instances severe and in others less obvious. English Stunt Virus and American Stunt Virus have drastically dwarfing and distorting effects on the plant, in a way which makes it impossible to be overlooked. By contrast, plants suffering from Virus B may grow on strongly and produce quality blooms though their leaves may exhibit patchy areas of darker and lighter colour, especially noticeable in the small plant early in the season. Where other viruses are present Virus B can intensify their effect.

Rogueing is therefore desirable at all phases of plant and bloom development. Unfortunately, a stock plant which is healthy one year may produce plants which are defective the next, for viruses can be transmitted from plant to plant by aphids and thrips, or in some cases as a result of plants being handled. The first indications can occur at the very beginning of the season, during the wintering of the stools. The odd stool may be found to carry cuttings which are yellowy, distorted and lacking in vigour. Such stools must be discarded. In other cases growths on a particular stool may appear "knuckled" and stunted, an obvious symptom of the bacterial disease Leafy Gall. Again the stool should be destroyed, for even the odd growth developing in apparent health and vigour will carry the disease.

While all plants taken from a particular stock plant may grow on healthily, or all may be defective, there are occasions where defects appear in only a percentage of plants. Just the odd plant may be chlorotic in foliage and reduced in vigour. Accordingly, small plants should be carefully culled before every potting or planting, even if it means growing less plants of a variety than was planned.

Other defects can become apparent as the season progresses. The fungus disease Verticillium, a serious wilt disease, can be carried over in cuttings from infected stock plants or it can be picked up from a soil or potting compost. The disease becomes apparent at about the time of bud development, leaves yellowing and withering relatively rapidly from the base of the plant upward. Plants infested with eelworm also become discoloured and blackened in the leaves from the base upward as the season progresses, but in this case with the discoloured areas distinctly V-shaped and bounded by the main leaf veins. While both disorders can be controlled and "clean" cuttings produced, the amateur is well advised to discard affected plants and where desirable to import new stock of the varieties.

On the other hand, some yellowing and withering of lower leaves is to be expected as stems harden, even where stock is healthy, but the upward progression of withering on healthy plants is slow and mostly confined to the hard lower stem below the point of emergence of the flowering laterals. The spread of both verticillium wilt and eelworm is more rapid and the effects more gross.

But the situation is not as daunting as it may seem. A sound and simple selection routine will effectively take care of most of the hazards, and the thoughtful amateur can run for seasons without serious problems. Fortunately, nurserymen also operate selection routines and, as a result, plants bought in are seldom defective.

The keen grower will automatically have his plants under scrutiny, with a thorough weekly – if not daily – inspection, and at the end of the season the plant producing the best results for the variety should be labelled "A", the second best "B", then "C" and "D". Other sound stools may also be wintered and cuttings from them may be needed, but doubtful stools must be destroyed and on no account used for stock purposes.

Some growers go as far as keeping only the best stool of each variety, but unfortunately a chosen stool may not produce enough cuttings, or it can break down in health in the stools period, and then we have to import new stock – which may be inferior to that which we discarded. Where differences in bloom quality are minimal and plant health is not in doubt it is far better to propagate from up to four sound stools, selecting where possible the bulk of the required plants from stool "A", but running reserves from stools "B", "C" and "D" in that order. If stock is basically sound, plants from the three reserves stools are then grown on if that from stool "A" breaks down or is insufficient for the season's needs.

It is sound policy to root twice as many cuttings of each variety as will be needed, with a view to selecting the strongest and healthiest at each phase of potting and planting. Batches of apparently equal cuttings do not always develop into equal plants and weaklings should be discarded. Careful selection should be part of every potting and planting, which means that spares should be carried. This eliminates most problems, and coupled to final thoughtful selection of stock plants at the end of each season makes for virtually troublefree growing. If six plants of a variety are to be planted out (in the case of earlies) or potted into finals (in the case of lates), root twelve cuttings wherever possible, plant several spares into first pots and at least one in second pots.

The Overall Aim

Having ensured that each small plant is raised from quality stock, it follows that at the beginning of the season every plant should be capable of producing the best possible blooms for the variety. But while our methods of cultivation may be capable of producing blooms of this desired high quality, they could equally fall short of the ideal. In fact, success or failure will depend first on quality stock, and second on the sort of plant we develop. If we produce the right sort of plant we shall succeed; if we do not we shall fail.

Left to its own devices a plant will develop roots, stems, leaves, buds and blooms in keeping with its genetic inheritance, eventually producing heads of bloom in the form of sprays at a time natural to the variety. In the hands of the skilled grower, however, it will bear fewer but larger blooms of improved quality, usually at an earlier date – and this is the purpose of planned cultivation!

What, then, is the ideal plant, what is the cultural pattern that we must follow to produce it, and what are the climatic conditions best suited to its development?

A convenient starting point for cultural considerations is the "dry weight theory", which declares that the dry weight of the bloom or blooms carried by a plant is relative to the dry weight of the plant. In other words, the only way to produce blooms of increased dry weight is to produce plants of increased dry weight.

We believe that it is more correct to say that the dry weight of the bloom (or blooms in the case of sprays) is relative to the dry weight of the lateral (flowering stem) which bears it (or them), rather than relative to the dry weight of the entire plant; therefore if we assume that the percentage of dry weight in a plant and lateral is a virtually fixed amount relative to moisture content, it would be logical to assume that where disbudded specimen blooms are concerned full-sized blooms can only emerge from full-sized laterals. This, in fact, constitutes a sound basis for cultural assessments. We are already beginning to build our basic pattern: varietal selection, quality stock, and now we see the need of full-sized laterals. We shall look to other considerations as we progress.

Size of bloom is, of course, only one quality requirement, but it is generally accepted that full-sized blooms, for the variety, are more desirable and more meritorious than small blooms, so long as they retain to the full all the other points of quality, such as rich colour, sleek form and crisp freshness. To hold these latter qualities while achieving peak size is the real challenge to the grower. In the following chapters we shall be proceeding step by step through the season with a view to producing full-sized blooms with all the other qualities. We shall be looking into the production of the desired long, strong laterals, into the important phase of bud development, and into the final opening of the bloom.

CHAPTER 2

Wintering Stools and Buying Plants

Numbers And Timing Of Growths

Practically, the first concern is to ensure that you have sufficient cuttings in rooting condition for the date of their requirement.

Some varieties produce many growths from below the soil ("basal growths") which are suitable for propagation, but others produce very few, and in some cases basal growths are virtually non-existent, and you will have to make use of shoots emerging from the main stem, called "stem cuttings".

Unfortunately, some growers are unjustifiably prejudiced against the use of stem cuttings. While the development of an ample supply of strong basal growths may be desirable, where they are in short supply stem cuttings can be used with every expectation of satisfactory results, especially where they emerge from the lower regions of the main stem. The reason for prejudice is that stem growths close to the flower head can have been subjected to the flowering impulse during the flowering season and as a result produce premature flower buds in their tips soon after rooting, failing to grow on in the desired way – but this is unlikely with growths from the basal regions of the main stem.

Ideally, stools growths should be no more than a few inches long when their tops are removed for use as cuttings. But many growths appear far too early, in some cases well before plants flower, and if they are left to develop they simply grow on as secondary stems producing a later crop of small flowers. Their blooms are inferior and they are of no use as cuttings. But they can be manipulated to build up increased stocks of cuttings for a later date. The tactics are simple. Allow such early growths to develop to, say, two inches in length then nip them back to soil level or, in the case of stem growths, to close to their point of origin, which will result in a later crop of secondary growths, usually two or three from each shoot, thereby increasing the number of available cuttings. The effect is similar to the "stopping" of a plant to produce several laterals. If you pull up unwanted early basal growths indiscriminately you remove a valuable source of next season's cuttings.

Basal and stem growths should not be allowed to become too

long before they are nipped back, for as they lengthen growths tend to harden at the base, and they may then fail to produce secondary growths. So nip them back while they are short and soft as a matter of routine.

So much for numbers. But you must also aim at timing growths, with a view to their being a few inches long on the date required. This calls for final trimming of stools on a date calculated to allow just enough time for the formation and development of growths. Speed of development is obviously an important consideration. Under controlled commercial conditions one could work to precise dates, temperature levels and cultural routine, but the amateur has to be approximate, and this is generally quite sufficient. With lifted stools of earlies wintered at low temperatures one should allow in the region of twelve weeks between the final trim and the date of cuttings insertion, while ten weeks should be sufficient for lates left undisturbed in their pots. At the time of the final trim all but small growth just showing through the soil should be trimmed back to just above soil level.

Earlies are frequently given their final trim just before lifting, and this suffices in the majority of cases, but where very early rooting is needed for an early stop the final trim will need to be carried out some weeks prior to lifting. We shall be dealing with "timing" in detail in a later chapter.

Lifting And Boxing Stools Of Earlies

The three main enemies of wintering stools are frost, slugs and excessive moisture, and the only way to bring stools of earlies through the winter satisfactorily is to trim and lift them and accommodate them in a cold frame or greenhouse, preferably the latter, where the main hazards can be conveniently countered.

Earlies stools should be lifted toward the end of October or early in November, before damaging frosts are experienced. They can be boxed, planted in a bed on the greenhouse staging or planted direct into the bed of the frame. The routine adopted will depend on facilities, but boxing is the most popular method. Boxes should be 4 in to 5 in in depth. Where they have been in use before, they should be sterilised by washing in a general-purpose garden disinfectant, say Jeyes Fluid mixed at a tablespoon to two gallons of water. Where suitable greenhouse accommodation is available, and bedding direct on to the staging is planned, the staging should be fitted with 4 in or 5 in edging boards.

Prior to lifting, stools should be stripped of all upper greenery, and where final trimming has not already been carried out all but tiny basal growths just emerging from the soil should be trimmed to soil level. The main stem should then be cut down to about 6 in with a sharp pair of secateurs. Though some growers lift stools variety by variety, labelling only the "A", "B", "C" and "D" stools, it is far more foolproof to tie a short label to each stool with the name of the variety and "A", "B", etc., details before lifting.

Lift each stool gently with a garden fork. Some of the soil will fall away in the process, but as much as possible of the remainder should be teased away from the roots with the point of a label. Next immerse the stools for a few minutes in clean water, then swish the roots carefully through the water to dislodge as much of the remaining soil as possible. On removal, trim straggly roots back to a diameter of, say, 4 in to 5 in, then immerse completely for two or three minutes in Jeyes solution mixed at a tablespoon to two gallons of water, or in some other mild garden disinfectant. On removal, lay them out for a short period for surface moisture to evaporate.

Washing and sterilising rids the roots of worms, slugs, and their eggs, and ensures a clean pest-free start to the new season. Both disbud and spray varieties should be treated in the same way.

The bedding material can consist of John Innes No. 1 potting compost, seed compost, or one of the soilless composts, but as a simple alternative even washed stools can produce satisfactory crops of cuttings in a mixture of equal parts peat and horticultural sand. The material used must be free of soilborne pests and diseases, and for this reason garden soil should not be used.

Where stools are to be bedded in boxes place an inch or two of the bedding material in the bottom, position the stools so that the trimmed roots just touch, then work more bedding material between them until they are set slightly deeper than the old soil level with labels facing to the front. The procedure is exactly the same where stools are bedded on the greenhouse staging. Note that seed trays are not deep enough for chrysanthemum stools.

Where rows of stools are to be bedded on the floor of the frame, it is advisable to soak the undersoil a week or so beforehand with a mild Jeyes solution, and in all cases where frames are to be used for accommodating stools, whether bedded or in boxes, the inside of the frame should be washed down with Jeyes, and slug bait should be put down to account for any unwelcome guests.

Lates Can Be Left In Their Pots

Lates can be bedded or boxed when they have flowered exactly as for earlies, or they can be left undisturbed in their pots. The latter is the more usual, but where space is limited some growers do box them. Whether in boxes or pots, they should be wintered throughout on the greenhouse staging. In many cases the final trimming of basal growths will have been carried out before the end of flowering, the final trim being some ten weeks before cuttings will be required.

Figure 2.1 Earlies Stools Trimmed and Sterilised Ready for Boxing

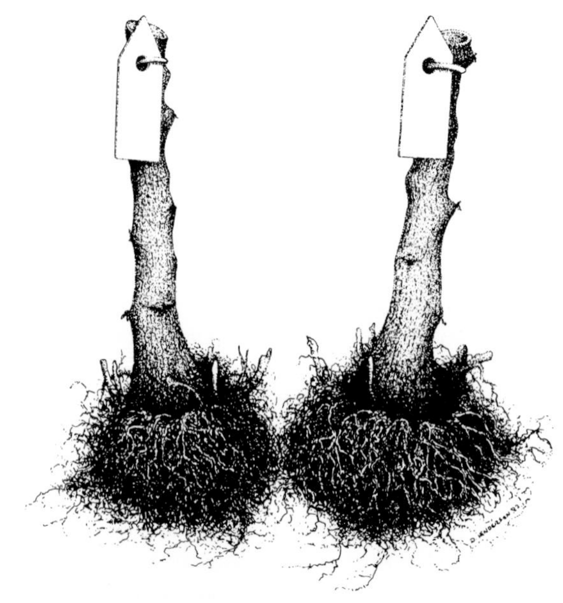

Figure 2.2 Tray of Stools Carrying a Crop of Cuttings

Where lates are boxed or bedded the main stem can be cut down to 6 in, but where they are left undisturbed in their pots the uptake of moisture will still be appreciable, and this can lead to sap bleeding from the top of the stem. So, with stools left in their pots, leave the main stem 12 in to 18 in in length, and if bleeding subsequently occurs ease the roots carefully out of the pot and let them resettle: this tends to reduce moisture uptake and counter the bleeding. As with earlies, label stock stools "A", "B", "C" and "D".

Winter Treatment

Trimmed stools are at first so many stems protruding from the compost or bedding material, especially in the case of replanted stools of earlies. They must, however, still be treated as living plants. Growth buds will already be developing and one severe frost could ruin the season. In a few weeks' time growths will be developing, but nothing should yet be done to hasten them. The aim until the turn of the year, except where very early cuttings are required, is simply to keep the stools alive and healthy but ticking over slowly.

In some cases boxed stools of earlies will be spending the early weeks in the frame, prior to transfer to the greenhouse; where bedded or where boxed and no greenhouse is available they will be wintered throughout in the frame. But first let us consider the routine where stools are accommodated in the greenhouse throughout.

After the housing of boxed earlies or the final trimming and cutting down of lates in their pots apply liberal ventilation by day in all but strong wind, frost and fog, with a temperature of 40°F to 45°F by day and 35°F to 40°F at night. This is quite high enough, though the day reading is bound to rise in mild spells and bursts of sunshine. An unexpected drop to 30°F on the odd night will do no harm – chrysanthemum sap does not freeze until the temperature drops to 28.5°F – but avoid severe frosts. These are economic temperature levels. Furthermore, if the greenhouse is "double glazed" with a polythene lining the heating bill will be halved, in addition to which the smaller amateur house will be much more pleasant to work in during the winter months. A small unlined house can be very chilly round the shoulders in icy spells!

Ventilation is an art, and not just a matter of throwing open a door or window. This is especially so with a small structure. The door and/or ventilators should always be adjusted to provide a gentle air circulation, avoiding strong drying currents and draughts. A gradual change of air is all that is necessary when it is cold, but wider ventilation is desirable to cool the house when it becomes excessively warm.

Bear in mind that the purpose of ventilation is not just to control temperature. It is just as necessary to control humidity and to avoid the extremes of very damp and very dry atmospheric conditions. Try to keep near to the desired temperature levels and to a reasonable level of humidity. It is sometimes said that a "buoyant atmosphere" is desirable, but it is impossible to define this exactly. Perhaps the best advice is to avoid extremes. Mastery of the art and assurance will come with experience.

The amount of ventilation provided depends largely on temperature, wind velocity and the size and position of the greenhouse. Generally speaking, you need less ventilation at low temperatures. The same applies in windy weather, and a small greenhouse operates with a smaller ventilating area than a large one; likewise a greenhouse in an exposed, windblown position relative to a similar structure in a more sheltered situation. Ventilation should always be applied away from the wind, for if the wind blows directly into an opening, plants can be subjected to an unhealthy, chilling airflow. This can be a problem in small houses with only one roof vent, but if butter muslin is pinned over the opening, air will filter gently through the mesh. Side vents should be used with caution, if at all, during the winter and spring periods where stock is accommodated on the staging.

The temperature levels suggested may seem low, but where final trimming is ten to twelve weeks ahead of cuttings requirement, growths should reach the desired length in good time.

Some form of heating will be needed, of course, and there are a number of alternatives – solid fuel, gas, electricity, paraffin, propane and butane gas. Cost of heating is a common concern, but in the case of wintering chrysanthemums we can operate economically. First, temperature requirements are low; second, heating costs can be halved by lining the greenhouse with sheets of polythene. Though each of the alternatives can be used effectively, electric fan heaters are best wherever a supply can be conveniently provided, with paraffin as a popular second choice.

Electricity is clean, and thermostats can be set at the desired level to trip on and off within a few degrees of the setting with minimum waste; and with electricity in supply the fitting of lights follows automatically, making it easier to work in your greenhouse in the evening should the need arise. Electric fan heaters need no maintenance except an occasional few spots of oil.

Where heating is by paraffin a small amount of ventilation must be provided when the lamp is in use, for flames need a supply of oxygen, and burned gases must be able to escape. Try to maintain a very gentle air circulation: a little air filtering in to the lamp, then circulating round the house to escape to atmosphere by way of a ¼ in or so of space through a roof vent – conveniently for oil lamp users, cold air falls and warm air rises. The burners of oil heaters should be set to burn brightly. A low, lazy flame produces fumes, but if the burners are set too high flat-wick lamps will smoke and blue-flame types may go out. Blue-flame heaters are recommended wherever practicable. In either case wicks must be kept clean, and they should be trimmed at least once a week through the winter period. Water trays are sometimes provided with paraffin heaters. They should not be used for chrysanthemums. Oil lamps discharge unwanted water into the atmosphere as oil is burned, and the more water vapour which escapes through the roof vents the better.

Not Too Moist To Begin With

Except where early cuttings are needed, stools should be kept somewhat on the dry side in the pre-Christmas period, watering lightly only when the surface of the compost (in the case of pots) or bedding material (in the case of boxes) is becoming uniformly dry. Apply the equivalent of a level ¼ in of tap water at such times, then leave strictly alone until they begin to dry again. Overhead syringing should not be necessary.

But A Change Of Tactics In The New Year

The New Year heralds a gradual change of tactics. Stools already in the greenhouse will need watching to ensure that they are progressing steadily to the desired length by their rooting dates, and where boxes of stools have been kept back under cool treatment in the cold frames they will soon need housing to accelerate their rate of growth.

Growth is naturally slow up to the turn of the year, but even at the low temperature levels advocated the growth rate will gradually accelerate as the days lengthen, and it should not be difficult to produce a plentiful crop of cuttings of suitable length and in good, soft rooting condition for the second half of January. As we shall see when we consider propagation, cuttings in some cases will be needed for December, but this should be no problem if final trimming has been carried out at the correct time.

Where it becomes obvious that growths are backward, steps should be taken to speed them up. Nothing can be done about daylength, of course – at least not without knowledgeable extension of photosynthetic daylength – but growth can be hastened by bottom heat and by the use of nitrogenous feeds.

Under the chapter on propagation we shall be advocating the use of warmth beneath a greenhouse staging to assist rooting, and where such a staging has been prepared and warmed gently by electric cable heating or by an under-staging paraffin heater backward stools can be placed on it to speed their development. If such stools are then kept a little more moist and given a weekly drink with a quick-acting nitrogenous liquid feed they should begin to accelerate in growth. In fact, some growers give all their stools a feed a few weeks before cuttings are needed; this freshens growths and softens them, leading to speedy and prolific rooting. Hard cuttings are slow to root and they produce very few rootlets. Where feeds to stools are applied the ratio between nitrogen, phosphorus and potassium should be in the order of 3-1-1.

The number and character of growths varies considerably with varieties. Some produce only a few cuttings, but where they are tightly clustered and well in excess of requirements they could be thinned as they develop, removing weaklings and those which are in any way defective. But if growths are well advanced think twice before cutting them back to soil level with a view to a later crop. Except where growths are stout and vigorous, the second crop is invariably thin and weak to begin with at this time of the year, and it will be many weeks before they develop to rooting length.

Damping; Pests

Stools growths are sometimes attacked by harmful fungoids, and "damping" results. In other words, stems rot at or just below soil level. Such troubles are more likely where the bedding medium is kept excessively moist and where an unsterilised bedding medium has been used. If outbreaks occur, remove the damaged shoots and dust round the stool with a captan powder or some alternative fungicide.

Routine spraying with insecticides should not be necessary, but keep watch for aphids in growing tips and for leaf miner tunnels in leaves, and if they appear spray well with an appropriate insecticide on a sunless day. Never spray in sunshine, especially under glass. If stools of earlies have been washed off and sterilised, and if lates were clean at the time of stripping, there should be few troubles.

Stools In Frames

The management of stools kept throughout in frames is similar in principle to those in the greenhouse, but temperatures are lower and humidity will be higher. With protection in hard frost, however, stools will come through successfully, though rooting may have to be later. It may, for this reason, be necessary to reject varieties needing early rooting. Development can be hastened by the use of electric cable heaters or other heating methods, and this will be a further safeguard against damage by frost, but in their absence little can be done to promote early cuttings.

In fact, few keen chrysanthemum growers in temperate regions operate without a greenhouse, though many growers of earlies keep their boxes of stools in cold frames for the first weeks and take them into the greenhouse at the turn of the year to quicken the development of cuttings.

Frame management is largely a matter of thoughtful ventilation in all but frost, snow and dense fog, plus covering with sacking or matting in hard weather, more especially on frosty nights. In really hard spells stools can be covered with newspaper for a few days before the frame lights are drawn over and the sacking put on. Such hard spells are not common in the pre-Christmas period, and where boxes of stools are in the frame for only a few weeks the lights can be fully open by day in milder spells, and at least propped well open in other than frost.

Less water will be needed in frames than in the greenhouse. If the bedding material was nicely moist when the stools were planted they will run for many weeks without watering. Where stools are wintered throughout in the frame, however, water will be needed later in the stools period, especially as the days lengthen and growths begin to develop.

There is little danger of pests being really active in the low temperatures of the frame during the stools phase, but a watchful eye should be kept on shoot tips for the presence of aphids. A more likely danger is slugs, and it is sound policy to put down slug bait every few weeks. A few slugs can inflict serious damage on wintering stools.

Summing Up

Stools should be kept cool and on the dry side to begin with; ventilation should be generous in all but frost, snow, fog and strong, cold wind; only a minimum of artificial heat will be needed in the greenhouse; watering should be generous for a few weeks before cuttings are needed; keep watch for aphids and slugs.

Ordering Plants

While established growers produce most of their plants from their own stools, there are always exciting new things on offer in catalogues – and all with glowing descriptions! A season is undoubtedly more interesting if one has a few new varieties to look forward to, but they should be chosen thoughtfully. Pictures in catalogues give one a good idea of bloom characteristics and quality, and so, too, do the National Chrysanthemum Society's awards. But you will feel more certain if you have seen a variety at the shows. Order with assurance rather than by chance; send in your order promptly; arrange to collect your plants from the nursery if you can rather than have them sent through the post; ask for an early rather than a late delivery, then if the nurseryman is inundated and your order is unavoidably held up you should still receive your plants in reasonable time.

CHAPTER 3

Propagation

Newcomers to chrysanthemum cultivation frequently regard the rooting of cuttings as a mystic art. In fact, with experience it becomes one of the easiest of the year's activities, with failure rare. But there are many methods, some unnecessarily complicated. In looking for an effective personal routine it is as well to bear in mind that no-one ever rooted a cutting – all we do is keep them alive and healthy while they form roots of their own accord. But we can influence their speed of rooting and the number of roots they produce, and we can employ methods calculated to keep them hardy and healthy during the process. A further logical objective is simplicity as well as efficiency.

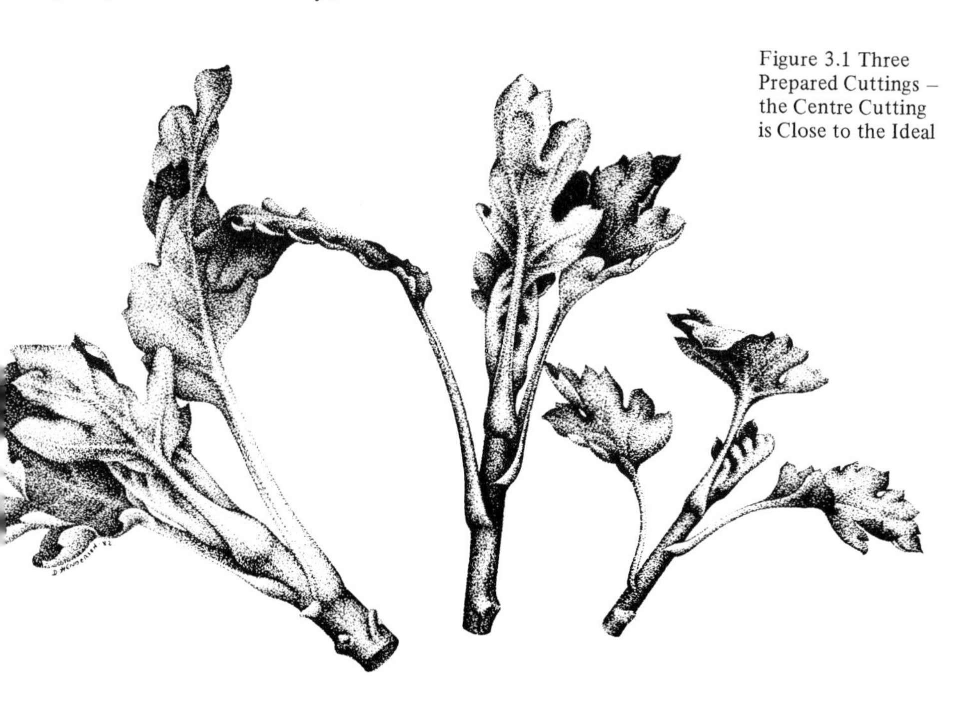

Figure 3.1 Three Prepared Cuttings – the Centre Cutting is Close to the Ideal

Two main factors govern the speed of rooting: the condition of the cutting and temperature. Fresh growths root more readily than those which have been slow in growth and have become hard in the stem. Cuttings should be in a state of active growth when removed from the stools. If they are semi-dormant, rooting will at best be delayed. Root development is also more rapid at high temperatures than low. At 70°F to 80°F roots will form on fresh cuttings in little over a week; at 40°F they will need six weeks or longer.

Where favourable rooting conditions are provided, hormone preparations do not appreciably hasten root formation, but in almost all cases they increase the number of roots formed.

These are basic facts and are important to bear in mind.

When To Root – Link With Stopping Dates

Cuttings may be inserted any time between November and April for disbud cultivation, and even into July in the case of late-flowering sprays.

For conventional purposes, rooting should be dated to ensure that a plant will have time to develop to "stopping condition" on the stopping date planned for the variety, i.e. with the embryo shoots visible in the leaf axils (see Chapter 7), or with the "break bud" developing in the growing tip at the desired time. Although the period between the insertion of cuttings and the plant reaching the ideal stopping condition varies with the variety and with climatic and cultural conditions, an average guide is to insert cuttings twelve to sixteen weeks ahead of stopping dates. The longer period is allowed for cuttings inserted in the short days of winter when growth is slow, and the shorter period for those inserted when the days are lengthening and growth begins to quicken. In warm climates the period is often considerably reduced.

The Respective Sections

The first cuttings inserted are those of late-flowering specimen plants – usually in November.

Large exhibition and medium exhibition varieties follow, beginning in December for those requiring an early stop and running through to February for later stops, and to March for any flowered on the break bud. These massive blooms take five weeks or more to develop, and relatively early buds are needed if they are to produce mature blooms on a given date.

Late-flowering incurves, reflexes, intermediates and singles are normally inserted from mid-January to mid-February, again depending on the stopping date, but with a few being inserted in March.

When grown as earlies, October-flowering varieties are inserted in late January or early February to provide for an early stop and the completion of flowering before the first frosts. Insert in March for a later stop for flowering in November.

Early-flowering (outdoor) varieties are normally inserted between early February and mid-March, depending again on the stopping date. Some require only a short season of growth and need a later stop; some have a longer period between the stop and the bud, with stopping and rooting needing to be advanced for blooms on a particular date. Early sprays are generally rooted either in late February or early March.

Late-flowering sprays are inserted either in mid-June where a stop is to be applied for each plant to produce, say, three sprays, or in mid-July where they are to be flowered "straight up" without a stop.

Delay In Hard Winters

So much for ideals. In most cases, where final trimming and management has been as recommended growths will be long enough for rooting and moving steadily forward on the date of their requirement, but in exceptionally hard weather they may not be sufficiently advanced. In such cases it is better to postpone rooting. It is far better to have a strong fresh growth a few weeks after the planned date than to insert short semi-dormant shoots in rigid adherence to the calendar. Hard spells do not last for ever, and as the days lengthen growth will quicken.

Basic Needs

The needs of rooting cuttings can be readily stated. They need moisture to prevent them dehydrating; they need a reasonable temperature level to encourage the metabolic processes within the plant which lead to the production of roots; and they need oxygen to keep stem tissues healthy and to assist with root development. The medium in which cuttings are rooted should therefore be aerated and yet reasonably moisture retentive, and it should be "warm".

We have experimented with many rooting mediums: pure sand, peat and sand, John Innes composts, brick chippings, vermiculite, pure peat, and even water. But the most satisfactory in our opinion, and the one we have used for many years, is a mixture of equal parts of loam, peat and sand. This answers all the needs of rooting with virtually no problems. However, where desired, John Innes potting or seed compost is suitable, and so too is a mixture of equal parts of peat and horticultural sand. Perlite can be used as an alternative to the sand.

As we have seen, chrysanthemums root slowly in a medium kept at 40°F, but they root more speedily as the temperature is increased.

The ideal is 60°F to 65°F. At this level they will "root like twitch" in about two and a half weeks. Some means of keeping the bottom temperature at this level is therefore desirable.

Figure 3.2 Cuttings in the Bed on the Greenhouse Staging

The Ideal Amateur Method

The method best suited to the amateur is to turn one staging of a greenhouse into a rooting bench. Overlay the staging with asbestos sheeting and secure an electric cable heater to the asbestos at 3 in spacings, to cover the area of the staging. The staging should have a 4 in-deep surround board. Cover the cable with 2 in of moist builder's sand, and cover the sand with a sheet of stout polythene pierced with drainage holes. Then lay a 2-in bed of the loam, peat and sand rooting medium on the polythene ready for the cuttings. Some growers add a ¼ in overlay of horticultural sand, so that when a hole is made for a cutting some of the sand falls into the hole to provide a clean aerated seating. With the medium advocated here this is unnecessary.

Where possible, complete the arrangement by inserting a rod-type thermostat through the builder's sand over the heating cable; if this is then set at the desired level you have a virtually ideal rooting system. If a thermostat is not fitted, then a sound method of working is to switch the cable on overnight and off by day.

If heating is by paraffin, the greenhouse heater – preferably with a heat-distributing pipe – should be positioned under the staging to provide the desired bottom warmth.

Such a staging will have many uses. It can be used for bringing on backward stools, rooting cuttings, germinating pans of seeds, and later for keeping tomatoes happy in their first and second pots before they are transferred to summer quarters – and it operates economically!

For some years we rooted cuttings in elaborate glass-covered propagators, of varying design, simply because this was the traditional method. But glass covering and propagators as such are unnecessary for rooting chrysanthemums – in fact they are undesirable, for cuttings soften in their humid confines and then need careful weaning if foliar damage and checks are to be avoided. Where they are rooted on the staging in the more open atmosphere of the greenhouse, without secondary covering, they remain hardy, and foliar problems do not crop up.

Ideally, cuttings are snapped from the stools with the fingers at a length of about 1½ in, with no further trimming except for the removal of the bottom leaf. Fresh cuttings snap cleanly and root readily. This method is also less likely to spread any virus diseases from cutting to cutting than where stems are trimmed to length with a razor blade and virus-laden sap can be passed from one cutting to another by way of the blade. But where growth has been slow, cuttings may be too hard in the stem to snap cleanly, and here there is no alternative but to trim them to length with a blade. If this is necessary the blade should be wiped free of sap with a clean tissue after the cuttings from any one stool have been prepared, then sterilised by passing it through the flame of a small lamp before moving on to the next stool. Fussy? Maybe. But where valuable stock is concerned it could prove worth the extra few minutes the procedure takes.

The lower ¼ in of the stems is dipped in hormone rooting powder and the cuttings are then inserted into small holes made in the rooting medium to a depth of approximately ¾ in, and spaced two inches apart in rows two inches apart. Rows of holes can be made by means of a simple peg-board consisting of a strip of wood with 1-in dowels every 2 in, or by a small dowel dibber, or even a pencil butt.

We no longer advocate the dipping of the tops of cuttings into a combined insecticide/fungicide solution before insertion. Such dipping can lead to blindness or to the yellowing of foliage with susceptible varieties. It is far better to ensure that cuttings are kept free of pests and diseases as they develop. It is normally only the aphid that we need to control.

Figure 3.3 Inserting a Cutting in the Bed

When a batch of cuttings is complete water them well in with a drench from a fine-rosed Haws can, and repeat this watering every few days, and certainly as often as the surface of the bedding material begins to dry. Continue watering until rooting has taken place. This is in complete contrast to earlier teaching, but it is an essential part of this very effective propagation routine.

Although the recommended temperature of the rooting medium is 60°F to 65°F, the night air temperature in the greenhouse need be no higher than 40°F – again a distinctly economic level, especially where the greenhouse is lined with polythene. A level of 40°F is quite high enough; anything higher would be undesirable. Furthermore, normal greenhouse ventilation should be applied throughout the entire rooting period. Whenever the outside temperature is at 40°F or above the roof ventilators can be opened, with no inconvenience to the rooting cuttings – in fact it is to their advantage, for it ensures that they will remain desirably hardy and healthy.

The method of propagation we have outlined is similar in principle to that adopted by large-scale commercial establishments rooting cuttings by the tens of thousands on uncovered greenhouse stagings kept moist by frequent mist sprays. They employ such methods for very good reason: they are simple, economic, and very effective.

At the suggested temperatures rooting will take place two or three weeks after insertion, and after four weeks roots should be an inch or more in length, an ideal stage for potting up or bedding into deep seed trays and for transfer to the cool staging. They should not be left on the heated staging too long after rooting has taken place.

The system outlined is the one we believe to be best suited to the amateur. The polythene lining and low greenhouse temperatures keep costs down and plants healthy; the extra – and low cost – bottom heat leads to speedy rooting; the heated staging is the propagating bed, and the opposite cool staging accommodates the plants for a period after rooting. The system is orderly and effective.

Many growers are afraid that sunshine will damage rooting cuttings. The only time you need to provide shade is for late batches still rooting in March and April, and where late-flowering sprays are being rooted in June and July, when butter muslin can be used. Winter cuttings should never be shaded. Rooting cuttings always flag for a period, and in strong sunshine they may well appear to be in distress, but if the compost is kept nicely moist by the advocated fine-rosed waterings they will soon freshen and produce roots.

Where smaller quantities are involved growers sometimes prefer to root in seed trays or in small pots at, say, twenty-four cuttings to the tray or five round the inside of a 3-in pot. They root just as freely either way, so long as temperature levels and watering follow the standard routine.

Prevent "Legginess"

Sturdy plants are a source of pleasure to all growers, but all too often plants in first and second pots become "leggy", out of balance and certainly anything but impressive in appearance. We have used growth retardants to good effect for some years past, producing plants in the early stages which, frankly, have aroused considerable envy. Alar, B9 or some other hormone growth retardant should be sprayed over the rooting cuttings ten days after insertion and repeated every three weeks up to the time of stopping. This will ensure that the plants remain satisfyingly sturdy. The sprays should also be used on tall varieties later in the season as laterals develop, giving appreciable reduction in height.

Rooting Is Later In Frames

Frame operators with no greenhouse will need to modify their tactics and root a few weeks later, for the reason that stools growths are slower in development. If undersoil heating can be installed, the desired bottom warmth can, of course, be provided and rooting will then be relatively speedy, but where no heat is available rooting will take longer. Where frames are in use do not forget to renew the slug bait at intervals, and in country districts make sure that the odd field

Figure 3.4 Rooted Cuttings – Ready for Potting, Boxing or Bedding

Figure 3.5 Cuttings to be Rooted – Five to a Three-inch Pot

mouse cannot get into the frames – they love a winter and spring diet of juicy chrysanthemum shoots!

Figure 3.6 Cuttings Rooted in a Tray

CHAPTER 4

Composts and Soils

With the formation of roots and the need of potting or boxing we come to the important consideration of the world of the root. For consistent success by design rather than by good fortune it is useful to know how roots develop and operate, and what they need if they are to play their full part in the development of plants capable of producing high-quality blooms.

Roots should spread steadily throughout the entire growing season, in such a way that the plant gradually accelerates in vigour with leaves increasing in size as they ascend the stem, so that the outline of laterals when viewed from the side is that of a "long V". If you produce such laterals you will be well on the way to success, but this can only happen if the needs of the roots are fully met.

The only way to produce the right sort of plant with the right sort of laterals is by having the right sort of roots, which in turn means that you must have a properly constituted compost and, for earlies, a properly constituted soil. The old saying "What's on top is underneath and what's underneath is on top" is indeed profound. The desired build-up in the laterals can only be achieved if the plants have a healthy and steadily spreading root system in a fertile, mildly nutritive medium.

Physical Condition Our First Consideration

The condition of a soil or potting compost plays a vital role in the cultivation of the chrysanthemum. If the rooting medium is in poor heart peak results are impossible. Its physical constitution should be such that a healthy and adequate root system is encouraged, and nutrient supplies should be sufficient to sustain growth, without being excessive or unbalanced.

The desired physical state is secured by calculated additions to soils and by the careful selection and blending of potting compost materials. "Food" supplies are provided by the natural constituents of the mediums, by the addition of manures and fertilisers, and by feeding plants as they develop.

There are further considerations, for top-spit soil and potting composts are not the inert and lifeless masses that they are sometimes thought to be. Both are teeming with microscopic organisms, such as bacteria and soil fungi: some are harmful, some beneficial. A teaspoon of loam or top-spit soil contains millions of them. We must, of course, do what we can to encourage those which are beneficial and discourage those which are harmful, and to do this a reasonable level of aeration, moisture retention, warmth and soil "reaction" (the acidity/alkalinity level) is needed.

It is common knowledge that roots need moisture and that nutrient elements must be available to them, but roots must also have ample supplies of oxygen. In common with all living tissues, roots need oxygen for their metabolic functions and to assist with their intake of materials. Indeed, roots need oxygen for their survival, and if roots fail so does the plant.

Plants contain an internal air system running from the breathing pores of the leaves (called "stomata"), through the leaf ribs and stems. This supplies the necessary oxygen to most plant tissues, but it does not supply oxygen to young, active roots; their needs have to be met by external supplies from within the soil. Therefore, a soil must be adequately aerated, in addition to having moisture-retaining properties.

In fact, a healthy top-spit soil is not a solid medium. It is no more than 50 per cent solid, the other 50 per cent being filled with air and water. When water is applied the pore spaces will be momentarily saturated and little air will remain, but there should be enough larger pore spaces, and drainage should be sufficiently free, to ensure that after watering and after heavy rain at least 10 per cent aeration is maintained, the percentage steadily increasing as moisture further drains, evaporates or is taken in by the plant. A soil with considerably less than 50 per cent pore space will not encourage healthy root activity, and will therefore be incapable of producing the sort of laterals which plants must have if they are to produce peak-quality blooms. Back to the dry weight theory!

Our first concern when considering soils and composts should indeed be their physical constitution, their aeration and their ability to retain moisture and yet to drain freely and become quickly recharged with oxygen after water has been applied.

Soils vary considerably in their characteristics. Some are sandy and gravelly, draining freely, but limited in their retention of both water and nutrients; some are clay-based, retaining water well and holding appreciable reserves of nutrients, but being insufficiently aerated and poorly drained; others may be silty and so fine and powdery that they suffer the failing of heavy clay – reduced aeration – but lack its inherent nutrient reserves, an unfortunate combination. The latter also "cap" badly after watering.

In the case of sands and gravels moisture-retaining materials and nutrients must be added; clays will need aerating and draining by additions of bulky materials such as peat or manure, plus sand and grit if they are available; silts will need bulky aerating materials, plus nutrients. If in doubt with any heavy soil add more materials calculated to increase drainage and aeration.

The John Innes Standards Provide A Sound Basis

John Innes composts, resulting from exhaustive scientific experiments, provide us with a sound insight into the needs of roots – and it is such basic principles that we must fully understand if we are to become competent plantsmen producing quality chrysanthemums by design.

The John Innes formula for potting composts consists of seven parts loam, three parts peat and two parts sand (parts by bulk), plus nutrients and chalk. But it is not just a matter of so many parts of anything which can be loosely referred to as loam, peat and sand. The quality of the ingredients is strictly defined.

Quality Loams

Loams are mixtures of sand, silt and clay, plus plant and animal remains, together with a population of living organisms ranging in size from microscopic bacteria and fungi to larger insects and worms. Although loams vary considerably in composition – heavy clay loams, medium loams, lighter sandy loams – the term "loam" implies that the material so described is a fertile agent in which plants of high quality can be grown.

The ideal loam is turf loam taken from a mature fertile pasture which contains sufficient clay to be slightly greasy, without being sticky, when smeared between finger and thumb in a slightly moist condition. Such a material would be referred to as a "medium loam". Heavy plasticine-like loams, and those which are excessively sandy, chalky, silty or peaty are unsuitable.

Turves should be cut 4 to 5 in deep between April and June, when the grass is in active growth, and stacked to mature in readiness for use the following season. Stacking proceeds as follows: a layer of turf is laid as a base, with the grass downward; this is then covered with a two-inch layer of loose strawy manure, followed by a second layer of loam, then a sprinkling of chalk. For medium-heavy loams the amount of chalk, in ounces per square yard, for every nine-inch depth of loam should be: the desired pH of the loam (6.3) minus the actual pH of the loam being stacked (say, for example, 5.7), multiplied by 23 which in the above example gives:

(6.3 – 5.7) x 23
= 0.6 x 23
= 13.8 ounces of chalk per square yard

(see page 50 for pH details).
The sequence is repeated until the stack is complete – loam, manure, loam, chalk, and so on – the materials being thoroughly wetted with a hose as stacking proceeds, to encourage bacterial action and the decomposition of fibres. The combination of grass, roots and strawy manure will ensure an adequate and necessary humus content in the loam when the stack is sliced for use the following spring, and will further ensure the maintenance of a healthy bacterial population. Ideally, a loam will be slightly acid, and the chalk is added with the aim of bringing the pH up to approximately 6.3. A loam with a high pH is unsuitable, for it will tend to "lock up" certain of the nutrient elements, with adverse effects on plant growth.

The fact that a loam has grown good crops of grass is some assurance that it is capable of growing good chrysanthemums, that the bacterial population and humus content will be satisfactory, and that the medium will be of good "crumb structure" and well aerated. Experienced growers will go to great lengths and travel many miles to obtain loam of the desired qualities.

Peat Aerates And Retains Moisture

Peat is chosen as an ingredient of composts for the reason that it aerates the medium and yet holds appreciable reserves of moisture, decomposing only slowly, and therefore fulfilling these functions over a long period. Both sedge and sphagnum peats are satisfactory, so long as they are coarsely fibrous or granular, with composite "particles" grading from 1/8 in up to 3/8 in. Fine, dusty or greasy sedge peats should on no account be used, nor should fine, silky sphagnums; they would drastically reduce the aeration of the compost.

Sand Assists Drainage

What is known as the "sand" content of John Innes composts would be more correctly termed "grit", for the bulk of its particles should be between 1/16 in and 1/8 in in size. It should be "sharp" and angular rather than rounded or smooth, and should have been washed free of impurities. Fine, powdery materials, such as builder's sand and fine silver sand, are unsuitable, since they fill the air spaces, "clogging" the compost and causing lack of aeration. The correct material will aid both aeration and drainage. Where coarse sharp sand is difficult to obtain perlite may be used as an alternative.

The Ideal Mixture

Loam, peat and sand, of the specified qualities, in the proportions of 7 3 2, are calculated to be close to the ideal, in their physical constitution, for the development of healthy root systems. But so often the available ingredients fall short of the specified standards, with the loam too powdery, the peat too dusty and the sand too fine. Such mixtures are insufficiently aerated, and they consolidate even more under successive waterings. Roots cannot operate satisfactorily in them, and results are bound to suffer. The peat must be granular and the sand must be coarse, and where the loam fraction falls short of the ideal, or stacking was not possible, we must consider adding extra peat and sand to modify the formula to 7 4 3, or even to 7 5 4 in extreme cases. We must ensure the necessary aeration; it is better to have too much than too little.

The same principles apply to soils. They must be adequately drained and aerated, in exactly the same way as composts, and while it may be impracticable to prepare them to such specific standards, the principles laid down for John Innes composts can at least be heeded. Drainage and aeration should again be the first consideration, and if necessary extra opening materials should be worked in well before planting. The ideal soil has been said to consist of six parts sand, two parts clay, one part humus and one part limestone – certainly not a solid mix!

The pH Level

Having ensured the desired physical properties, the next concern should be the pH rating, the acid/alkaline level. This is the second important consideration, for at very low pH levels phosphorus, potassium, calcium, magnesium and molybdenum supplies are reduced, while at high pH levels it is iron, copper, zinc, manganese and boron which suffer.

The reason for this is that both soil particles and nutrients are possessed of electrical properties which cause nutrients to be attracted to and held by the soil. The soil could be looked upon as a magnet, and nutrients as objects capable of being attracted to it and held by it, the degree of attraction varying with the different nutrients. Similarly, the "magnetic" properties of the soil, and the degree to which each of the nutrients is held or released varies according to its pH, and it is these factors which combine to vary nutrient retention and availability.

Plant growth will suffer at low or high pH levels. In soils and loam composts pH 6.0 to 6.5 is regarded as the ideal, but in peat and sand ("soilless") composts the electrical properties are such that the ideal is lower, at approximately pH 5.0.

The pH range extends from pH 0.0 (extreme acidity) to pH 14.0 (extreme alkalinity). Neutrality in terms of acidity/alkalinity is pH

7.0, ratings below this being acid and above alkaline, which means that the ratings of pH 6.0 to 6.5 mentioned above are slightly acid, while pH 5.0 is more strongly acid. In practice there is a greater likelihood of a too high pH level than a low pH in loams and soils.

As with the loam stack, where a soil is too acid and the pH low the answer is to apply chalk or hydrated lime. The remedy is not so simple where a soil is alkaline and the pH is high. Additions of sphagnum peat will help, however, and so, too, will dressings of sulphate of ammonia where these are acceptable. Where loams for composts are concerned we select where possible a material with approximately the desired pH rating, or one a little more acid with a view to the necessary adjustment by the application of chalk.

Nutrients

The third important consideration is nutrition. Some twelve elements are needed by plant roots, chief among them being nitrogen, phosphorus and potassium, together with calcium, magnesium, iron, sulphur, manganese, copper, zinc, boron and molybdenum. Sodium is also needed by some plant species, and chlorine has also been found to be an essential. The quantities involved are not appreciable, but each element is nevertheless necessary for healthy plant development.

Nutrients become available to the plant at different rates, depending on the form in which they are applied. It matters little to the plant whether they are applied in organic or inorganic, powder or liquid form. What is important is the rate and duration of their availability, and this should be considered whenever fertilisers are being selected.

Nitrogen is the "growth element", in that vegetative development increases whenever it is in adequate supply. It is the element most likely to be leached from the soil, and therefore the one most likely to need replenishing. The sources of nitrogen employed should therefore be carefully chosen. Hoof and horn, Gold N and Nitroform provide nitrogen steadily over a period; dried blood and urea are more quickly available over a shorter period; sulphate of ammonia and nitrate of ammonia are even more rapid in action.

Phosphorus plays an important role in the development and activities of young roots and young growth, and in many of the important metabolic functions of the plant. It is inherently abundant in some soils, but is held and released only gradually over a period of many seasons. Although a soil may contain ample reserves of phosphorus, the plant may not, in fact, be able to obtain all that it needs, and for this reason fertilisers added to soils and composts should always contain a proportion of readily available phosphorus. Superphosphate is a relatively quick-acting yet lasting medium and could well be looked upon as the standard general-purpose phosphatic fertiliser. Potassium phosphate and ammonium phosphate provide for more rapid availability.

When adding phosphatic fertilisers as a surface dressing bear in mind that they are immediately precipitated and held in the top inch or so of the soil, and are therefore only available to roots near the surface. When mixed into a soil or compost before planting they will, of course, be available to lower roots.

Potassium operates as something of a balance to the effects of nitrogen, and as such is sometimes referred to as the "sunshine element", the reason being that it has a beneficial effect on the rate of synthesis of sugars, thereby helping to maintain a satisfactory "carbon-nitrogen ratio" within the plant, an important consideration with flowering and fruiting subjects which we shall be considering in more detail later. Sulphate of potash is the popular "safe" supplier of potassium, supplying the element relatively quickly, yet steadily, over a period. Potassium nitrate and potassium phosphate are favoured for quick-acting liquid feeds.

Calcium needs are largely taken care of by considerations of pH, with composts based on the John Innes formula automatically enjoying ample supplies. Where a soil has a slightly acid, neutral or high pH level it will contain all the calcium plants need; where the soil is acid add chalk or hydrated lime to make good the deficiency. Chalk is the favoured calcium additive for composts.

Magnesium is a constituent of chlorophyll, and is therefore necessary for the functioning and even the existence of the plant, though not needed in vast quantities. Magnesium is usually held in adequate reserves in clay soils, but tends to be deficient in lighter soils, from which it is easily washed away by heavy rain. Serious shortage is unlikely where dressings of manure or vegetable compost are applied as part of the cultural routine or where good-quality loam is used as the basis of a potting compost, and many proprietary fertilisers contain magnesium. Magnesium sulphate (Epsoms salt) is the recommended supplier of the element, either for applying as a light dressing to soils or for use in liquid feeds.

Iron is not a constituent of chlorophyll, but the formation of chlorophyll can only proceed where it is present. Most soils and loams contain appreciable reserves. Iron deficiency within the plant, indicated by pale yellowing foliage at the growing tips, is more often due to its being made unavailable by high pH levels than to an actual shortage of the element in the soil. A soil may have plenty of iron in reserve, but high pH levels will prevent its release, and where such conditions apply further additions of, say, sulphate of iron will suffer the same fate: they will be locked up immediately they are applied. Where the pH is high and shoot tips become chlorotic, due to reduced iron availability, the remedy is to apply iron in "chelated" form. Sequestrene is a product which will correct such deficiencies, whatever the pH. But the better answer is to ensure that the pH of both soils and composts is close to the ideal.

Trace elements. The remaining elements, though necessary, are needed in only minute quantities, and are accordingly referred to as "trace elements". It is unlikely that additions of any one element would be needed where soils are maintained in fertile condition or where composts are based on fertile loams, and for practical purposes they are usually conveniently forgotten, though many proprietary fertilisers contain them in balanced quantities.

The Need Of Balanced Nutrition

Of all the nutrient elements, nitrogen figures most prominently, both in its effect on growth and in the amount taken in and utilised by the plant. But important though nitrogen might be, it needs to be balanced by potassium, phosphorus and all the other essential elements. Excessive nitrogen will in fact, lead to large plants but poor blooms which can damp badly. We need to strike a balance between the two extremes of gross rampant growth on the one hand and restriction and semi-starvation on the other. The same principles apply to the other elements: enough is needed but not too much, and in some cases "enough" is a very small quantity.

In practice, establishing a reasonable working balance is not as difficult as it may seem, for nearly all nutrients are absorbed by the soil to a greater or lesser degree and released only gradually for uptake by the plant. A soil may be relatively rich in an element, such as phosphorus or potassium, and yet be in only moderate supply to the plant. The fact that nutrients tend to be held in reserve and released gradually provides us with a safety margin and insures to considerable degree against unbalanced growth or damage to the plant.

Clay-based soils, in particular, have a considerable capacity for the storage and steady release of nutrients. This is why, when adequately aerated and containing ample humus-forming materials, they constitute the important basis of high fertility in a soil. By contrast, the coarser-grained sands and silts have little storage capacity and nutrients are more easily leached from them.

John Innes Nutrients

John Innes composts, based on quality loam which has been stacked with manure and allowed to mature, are calculated to contain ample supplies of most of the nutrient elements, and only nitrogen, phosphorus and potassium are added, plus chalk to balance the pH and to assist with the activation of the superphosphate in the base fertilisers. John Innes base fertiliser consists of:

2 parts hoof and horn – 1/8 in grist
2 parts superphosphate
1 part sulphate of potash
(parts by weight)

4 oz of base fertiliser, plus ¾ oz chalk, are added to each bushel of compost when preparing John Innes No. 1; 8 oz of base plus 1½ oz chalk for John Innes No. 2; 12 oz of base plus 2¼ oz chalk for John Innes No. 3. The composts are ready for use immediately after mixing.

Sterilisation

A further consideration is hygiene. Strictly speaking, the loam fraction of John Innes composts should be steam sterilised before the compost is mixed. The object is to eliminate pests and disease organisms by maintaining a temperature throughout the loam of 180°F for ten minutes. This is the approved method of sterilisation, but an alternative method some growers use is the soaking of the loam with Jeyes Fluid solution or some other disinfecting agent. But many experienced chrysanthemum growers working with familiar loams do not resort to any form of sterilisation, and they consistently produce blooms of the highest quality. John Innes composts supplied by horticultural sundriesmen will have been sterilised in the approved manner. Soilless composts need no sterilising.

Many growers of earlies have never felt the need of soil sterilisation, but both chemical and gas sterilisation can be resorted to, though the latter method is normally carried out by specialists.

Soilless Cultivation

It helps to put the roles of soils and composts into perspective if we consider hydroponic cultivation, the growing of plants in aerated water to which nutrients have been added. Fine plants and crops can be produced in this way. What this teaches us is that all that plant roots really need is water, the essential nutrient elements and oxygen. Everything else is a superfluous incidental which the plant could well do without. This is further indicated by the wonderful results enjoyed by so many growers of chrysanthemums in soilless composts, for the use of soilless composts is in principle closely akin to hydroponics. Most soilless composts are based on peat and sand, or just peat alone, which themselves supply virtually nothing in the way of nutrients. Plants grown in soilless composts rely on added nutrients, the appreciable air content of the medium, and water.

The practical value of soils and loam composts, and to a lesser degree soilless composts, is their ability to retain nutrients and to release them gradually over a period. But again composts must be adequately aerated. Many growers have found that their results have improved dramatically on changing from loam to soilless compost, due almost entirely to increased air at the roots. This is especially so where poor-quality loams were previously in use and composts were too fine and powdery. Further details of soilless composts can be found in the British National Chrysanthemum Society's publication *Growing Without Soil* by Dr Barrie Machin.

Pot Plants

Plants in pots are to a certain extent growing under artificial conditions. Requirements are basically the same as in a fertile open soil, but the root run of the plant is restricted to the small volume of compost contained by the pot. The compost, therefore, must be carefully prepared if it is to answer all the plant's needs and produce peak results.

It must remain aerated and drain freely, yet retain sufficient moisture to sustain the plant for a reasonable period; it should not become muddy when watered, nor cake on the surface when drying out; food supplies must be concentrated, yet in gradually available form; it must be neither excessively acid nor alkaline, and must maintain a satisfactory pH balance.

Opinions differ as to what constitutes the best blend for chrysanthemums. A witchdoctor's potion is nothing compared to some of the older recipes. Many of them were well reasoned and highly successful in expert hands, but they often included "magic" ingredients, the purpose of which many of their adherents appeared not to fully understand.

Why resort to a complicated formula when a simple one gives equal, and in some cases superior, results? Furthermore, ingredients of complicated recipes are often subject to wide variation, sample for sample, and results may vary accordingly. By contrast, properly prepared John Innes composts are standardised and capable of producing chrysanthemums of the highest possible quality season after season. Where quality loam cannot be obtained seek a quality ready-made compost, and if in doubt open it up with a little more peat and grit – or use a soilless compost.

Soil Preparation

The principles and practical applications of John Innes composts, and the lessons of hydroponic cultivation, provide a sound basis for controlled cultivation and at the same time give valuable guidance in matters of soil preparation. Clearly the needs of roots in open soils are exactly the same as in pots or under hydroponics, but circumstances are different, in that we are endeavouring to mould an *in situ* medium which may be far from ideal into something close to the ideal.

Soil is a mixture of mineral fragments and animal and plant remains. The mineral fragments vary in constitution, and in size from stones and gravel down to sand, silt and clay. Stones, gravel and sand keep a soil open, aerated and well drained; the smaller particles, clay in particular, make it compact, induce conditions of good moisture retention and hold reserves of plant nutrients. The clay fraction forms a kind of soil bank, in which surplus nutrients may be deposited for future use and from which other elements can be obtained in exchange. From a nutritive point of view it is the most important part of the soil, for the clay fraction alone supplies certain mineral elements required by the plant. Ideally a soil would contain sufficient larger particles to ensure good drainage and aeration, and sufficient smaller particles to facilitate moisture retention and ensure the steady availability of nutrients.

Soils differ greatly in their makeup. One authority writes of "no fewer than 179,001,000 different kinds of earths". For our purpose we need only consider the main soil groups, clays, sands, silts, chalks and peats, and whether they are too compact, too open, too moisture retentive and so on. Where we find an undesirable extreme, such as undue compaction and minimal aeration, we must endeavour to bring about the desired changes. Chrysanthemums will not flourish in plasticine-like clay or powdery silt; nor will they appreciate an impoverished sand or an acid peat. But a well-aerated and nutritive loam at the desired pH level will be capable of producing fine plants and fine blooms.

In many cases fibrous materials are needed to aerate and/or improve the moisture-holding properties of soils, and for this reason animal manures and vegetable compost are traditional and valued additives, in that they help to retain moisture and yet assist with aeration. At the same time they provide nutrients and humus.

Humus, a necessary ingredient of a fertile soil, as well as of loams, is a dark jelly-like substance of minute proportions which coats soil particles, retains moisture and holds the particles together in what are referred to as "soil crumbs". When we speak of the "crumb structure" of a soil we are, in fact, referring to the granulation of its particles in the presence of adequate humus, a highly desirable condition in terms of soil fertility. A soil containing adequate humus will be dark, crumbly, aerated, moisture and nutrient retentive, and generally fertile; a clay with little humus will be sticky and intractable, while sands with little humus will resemble those of the desert and seashore, with no crumb quality and no prospect of producing quality plants – except by hydroponic techniques. So humus is a necessary constituent of all soils.

Animal manures and vegetable composts are not a form of instant humus, however. Humus is created from them in the soil by its population of fungi and bacteria, and for this reason it takes time to turn barren land into a high level of fertility.

We are all familiar with a soil's visible population, such as worms, millipedes and centipedes, but soils are also teeming with creatures and organisms so minute that they can be seen only with the aid of a microscope. A teaspoon of fertile top-spit soil contains countless millions of them, some harmful, but mostly beneficial, and all playing their part in maintaining the soil's fertility. It is said that the micro-organisms of the soil "carry on such fierce activity on each acre that they expend an amount of energy equal to 10,000 beings living and working there". It is such activity which reduces organic material to humus and releases nutrients for uptake by the plant. Fibrous tissues, such as straw and fibrous roots, constitute the important long-term source of humus. Fresh, watery vegetable matter rots down more quickly and releases any nutrient content more readily, but supplies little of long-term benefit to the soil. Such factors should be borne in mind when bulky soil additives are under consideration.

Humus breaks down and disappears steadily, and therefore supplies of organic matter calculated to provide humus need to be added to the soil periodically. Well-rotted animal manures are deservedly in demand for the purpose, with properly prepared garden compost a useful alternative. Superb National-winning chrysanthemums have been produced on a plot that is never manured but dressed each year with garden compost – but no chrysanthemum debris should be used when making compost, to avoid any chance of passing on pests and diseases. Such bulky manures constitute an important source of food for the soil's organisms, and adequate supplies ensure a healthy soil population and increase fertility.

Having looked to principles, where do we begin? Again, we look first to soil condition, then to pH, and then to nutrient content. It could be said that if a soil is sufficiently fertile to produce quality vegetables it will be capable of producing quality chrysanthemums, and such a soil should be able to maintain that ability on an annual dressing of no more than a barrowload of well-rotted manure or garden compost to three or four square yards. But less fertile soils could be given double the dressing to improve their physical structure.

Some of the best growers of earlies simply lay manure on top of the soil in the form of an autumn top dressing, following routine digging, then fork it in early in the spring. This is satisfactory with fertile and open sandy soils, but more solid clays should have the manure dug in and be thrown up rough for winter frosts to break them down to a tilth. Again, the aim is to produce a reasonably open, aerated medium calculated to encourage healthy root action.

Heavy soils which tend to drain slowly and remain damp will be in need of special consideration and extra opening material should be worked into them, for preference at two spits deep instead of the more usual one. Where soils are heavy and drainage is poor, sandy and gritty materials are also a desirable additive, but they are seldom available in the desired quantities.

The pH of a soil is just as important as that of a compost, and tests should be made each year to establish the possible need of correction. A pH level of approximately 6.3 would be looked upon as ideal. It should not be above 7.0. Lime should be applied only if it falls below 6.3. Many soils do not need lime and it is wrong to dress them annually as a matter of routine. We have used a plot which has grown prize-winning earlies for close on 20 years with no more than a light sprinkling in the early years. Simple tests can be carried out with inexpensive test sets available from horticultural sundriesmen.

As we saw earlier, the lowering of the pH is somewhat more difficult. Applications of peat are helpful, and sulphate of ammonia when used to supply nitrogen is also beneficial (see p. 51).

A satisfactory arrangement is to dig during the autumn and to test for the need of lime early in the New Year, though where dressings of manure are laid over the surface after digging it will be necessary to check the pH soon after the stools have been lifted, before digging and manure spreading are carried out.

Fertile soils – the sort of soils capable of producing good vegetables – can be assumed to carry a reasonable supply of most of the essential nutrients, but a "base dressing" containing nitrogen, phosphorus and potassium raked in to the surface layers at, say, 4 oz to the square yard a few weeks before the earlies are planted is calculated to get plants off to a good start and to ensure sturdy development.

While soils and composts need to be adequately supplied with nutrients, they can be too rich. A well-aerated medium of moderate nutrient content will encourage strong root action and strong lateral development, yet with the plant in the condition necessary for the development of quality blooms. Rich soils encourage strong vegetative development, but with stout, pithy stems and large bloated leaves. Such plants may look impressive in terms of their bulk, but they will not produce peak-quality blooms. The basic nutrient content of John Innes composts is quite sufficient for our purposes for pot plants, and little feeding would be necessary were it not for the limitations of root development imposed by the pot. Soils need to be no richer in terms of their nutrient content, and due to their unrestricted root-run even less feeding will be needed.

We shall be looking further into the subject of nutrition as the season progresses. But from the start we should bear in mind that we are producing flowers, and that their nutritional requirements are subtly different from those employed for the production of leafy vegetables.

If the fertility level of your soil is in doubt seek further advice. There are specialist organisations which offer soil test facilities, and most counties operate horticultural advisory services and should either be prepared to undertake a soil test for you or at least advise you of local facilities.

To conclude, bear firmly in mind:

(a) the need of the appropriate physical constitution, with good drainage and aeration, yet with adequate moisture retention;
(b) the need of a satisfactory pH level;
(c) the need of a steady and balanced supply of nutrients.

CHAPTER 5

Potting Up and Hardening

Cuttings will be due for potting up a week to ten days after marked signs of freshening. At the recommended rooting temperatures one could plan for potting into 3½ in-pots four weeks after the cuttings were inserted, by which time roots should have developed to an inch or so in length. An ideal medium for the purpose is John Innes No. 1 compost. We use loam composts for first and second pots, followed by either loam or soilless for final pots for lates, but some very successful growers use soilless composts throughout.

A bushel of compost will pot in the region of 90 plants: a hundredweight will pot half as many again. Pots must be clean and dry when used, so wash and sterilise them well in advance, using Jeyes solution at two tablespoons per gallon or a similar general-purpose garden disinfectant.

The Day Before Potting

Water rooted cuttings the day before potting and check that the necessary materials are at hand. The potting operation is simple. Place a half-inch of peat in the bottom of the pot, and then fill to about an inch from the rim with loose compost. As far as practicable roots should then be spread over the surface of the compost, and further compost added to fill the pot, followed by gentle consolidation with the fingers. Add a label and the operation is complete. Potting up is no more complicated than this. Note that no crock is needed in the bottom of the pot.

But there is one other important consideration, namely the moisture content of the compost at the time of potting. A parched compost is difficult to moisten thoroughly after potting and can lead to root damage, while an overmoist compost can become compressed during potting with aeration drastically reduced and root action impaired. Whenever potting, boxing or bedding is carried out a compost should be just moist enough to hold together when squeezed in the hand, but when the hand is opened and the back of the hand is given a sharp rap the squeezed compost should break apart. If too dry apply a light sprinkling of water and mix thoroughly; if too moist mix with drier compost or lay out to dry well in advance of potting. Root action is indeed so very important at all stages and every effort should be made to ensure that the physical construction of composts is maintained and that roots are healthy and vigorous. Where the compost is in the correct condition – and it should be – watering-in will not be necessary.

Figure 5.1
A Well-established Plant in its First Pot

Stock selection is in operation even when potting up rooted cuttings. Some cuttings always root more freely than others, and consequently they get away to a better start and are obviously the ones to use – pointing to the wisdom of running spares of each variety.

An alternative to potting preferred by some growers is to plant in boxes 3 in to 4 in in depth with plants at approximately 6 in spacings.

Into The Frames

Plants should remain on the cool staging with maximum ventilation until mid-March, when in most districts it is safe to put them in the cold frame for the final stage of hardening. Later batches potted up in March should be given ten to fourteen days on the cool staging before transfer to the frame. With the sun gaining strength and the confines of the greenhouse becoming increasingly warm the best place for small plants is undoubtedly the cold frame, and in all but extreme weather they soon begin to freshen and show their appreciation.

While coddling is to be frowned on, plants should never be subjected to drastic climatic changes, especially following root disturbance, and hardening should be carried out gradually over a period.

After transfer to the frame, the lights should be kept more or less closed for a few days, after which air is gradually increased over the following weeks, until the lights are fully open by day, and at a later date (and more gradually) fully open by night. Ventilation will need to be reduced temporarily in cold winds, the lights being tilted in such a way as to screen the plants from the airflow. In periods of night frost the lights should be closed down and covered with matting.

With cuttings rooting and earlier batches beginning to grow away and look important, this is one of the most enjoyable, yet one of the most tantalising periods of the chrysanthemum year, for invariably lengthening days with increasing sunshine are accompanied by cold, dry north-east winds, and to manage a small greenhouse and frames successfully in an exposed position under such conditions requires thought and care. While appreciable ventilation may be desirable to keep the temperature down the wind may be chill and the air excessively dry, and it is cold, dry air which damages tender tissues.

Remember that the admittance of quantities of cold, dry air means a drastic lowering of humidity; the result is a heavy increase in transpiration – in extreme cases beyond the tolerance of soft foliage. Remember, too, that an inch or two of air on a roof vent of a small greenhouse is equivalent to a fully open vent on a large house. Where young leaves have developed under greenhouse conditions there is a danger of damage to foliage if they are suddenly exposed to a cold dry atmosphere. It is better in such cases to employ moderate ventilation to maintain a reasonable level of humidity.

The ventilation of frame lights is best attended to by the use of wooden stepped "wedges" some 8 in x 6 in x 1 in thick with 1½-in steppings, which provide for graduated tilting of lights away from the airflow, either at the ends or at the sides, the amount of ventilation provided depending on the stage of hardening, temperature and the strength of the wind.

Figure 5.2 Frame Ventilation by Means of Stepped Wedges

Care With Watering

Watering now becomes an important consideration. If the compost was just moderately moist plants will need no water for at least a week. In fact, at this stage it is preferable to see plants begin to flag before they are watered, and then they should be given a good drink, say a level ½ in of water, then left until again in need. Water should not be given until the compost has begun to dry and the plant is on the point of flagging. As we have seen, it is important that roots are adequately aerated, and on no account should any plant be watered while the compost is still moist. These principles must be adhered to throughout the season. Thoughtful watering is an important cultural requirement.

Get into the habit of an early morning round – between sunrise and mid-morning – water all those in need without worrying too much about the weather being cold. If plants need water they must be watered, but again they must need water before it is given. Cold tap water is quite suitable for this and every other stage of chrysanthemum cultivation. The oft-advised use of rainwater is completely unjustified and in most cases equally impracticable. The great majority of prizewinning chrysanthemums are watered throughout straight from the tap.

Bedding As An Alternative

An alternative to pots for growers of earlies is to bed plants directly into the frames, in this case planting them into a 3 in bed of John Innes No. 2 compost at 6 in-spacings. Ideally, the compost will be placed on a 3 or 4 in bed of firmed ash from a coke stove or some other material which discourages dense root penetration and yet provides for an interchange of moisture.

The advantage, of course, is that pots are not needed and management is simplified. Instead of a daily round of watering, water must be restricted if rampant root action and undesirably gross development is to be avoided. Most growers employing the bedding method, with the compost and ash base in a nicely moist condition at the time of planting, do not water their plants at all until a few days before they are planted out on the open plot. Instead, they keep them moderately fresh with overhead sprays of clear water.

Keep Watch For Pests

With the commencement of the frame period insecticide sprays will soon be needed, for the leaf miner fly will shortly be visiting the plants, and so, of course, will the aphid. The presence of the former is often first indicated by the appearance of tiny pale specks on unfolding leaves, where the adult insect has been taking a meal or laying its eggs; aphids will at first appear in growing tips, where they can quickly build up in numbers. Try to give each plant a thorough individual examination each week, looking especially for attack by insects, and for the slime trails of slugs – with a consequent need to put down slug bait.

Imported Plants

Treat imported plants as if they had just come from your own rooting bed. In fact, they should be afforded extra consideration. Even where they have been collected from a nursery they will suffer a slight check, but if they have come through the post the check caused by root disturbance and travelling is considerable, and it usually takes a few weeks for them to become thoroughly established.

If roots are at all dry on arrival, stand them in water for an hour to revive them before potting up. Examine tips and leaves carefully for signs of pests and diseases and spray thoroughly if necessary. It is possible that they will have been more coddled than plants produced by the methods we advocate, and it is therefore advisable to keep them in a cosy corner of the greenhouse staging for ten to fourteen days, in this case providing light shading in strong sunshine until the roots begin to bite.

Spider

Spoon in Spray Form

Cascade

Bonsai

Medium Exhibition

Quill

Spoon

Bowl

(left) Intermediate
(bottom left) Single
(right) Large Exhibition
(bottom right) Spray

Incurve

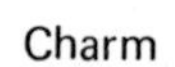

Charm

Floral Art

Reflex

CHAPTER 6

Potting On Into Second Pots

Young plants continue to develop steadily so long as the natural spread of the root system is not greatly impeded. It takes a few weeks, however, for the roots to completely saturate the soil ball and begin to twine round its outside. This is a crucial stage, for food supplies soon begin to fail. The plant continues to lengthen, but leaves become smaller and stem tissues harden; lower leaves begin to yellow and wither.

A badly checked plant never completely recovers, however considerate its later treatment. The lower stem will remain thin and hard, the flow of nutriment is impaired and development restricted. By contrast, a plant potted on into a larger bulk of compost at the correct time will progress without interruption.

When To "Pot On"

In practice, plants should be "potted on" into larger pots when roots have broken freely through the outside of the soil ball and are beginning to encircle the base. This is usually in the region of five or six weeks after the first potting. The inspection of root development should be a matter of routine some five weeks after potting.

To remove a plant from its pot for root inspection hold the pot in the palm of the right hand, place the left hand palm downward across the top of the pot with the plant stem between the middle and index fingers, turn the pot upside down, then, holding the bottom of the pot with the right hand and supporting the compost with the left, rap the rim of the pot sharply on the edge of the frame. The compost ball should slip from the pot cleanly without root disturbance. An important precaution: the compost ball must be moist. If it is dry roots will adhere to the inside of the pot, and root damage is inevitable. If necessary, water plants an hour or two before they are removed.

Prepare In Advance

Pots should be washed, sterilised with Jeyes Fluid if necessary and dried in advance, and compost should be prepared in readiness, assessing in particular its moisture content. One bushel will be sufficient to pot on approximately 50 plants from 3½ in to 5 in; a hundredweight will suffice for 75.

John Innes No. 2 is the compost we recommend, with 5 in as the most suitable pot size.

Figure 6.1
A Strong Root System Ready for Potting on into a Larger Pot

The Potting Procedure

The potting procedure is similar to that followed for potting up. Again, no crocks are needed. A one inch layer of peat in the bottom of the pot will prevent the compost falling through and ensure satisfactory drainage. Add an inch or so of new compost over the peat and firm gently. Remove any yellow or dried lower leaves from the plant to be potted, remove its label and tap it from its pot. Position the old compost ball centrally in the new pot on sufficient loose compost to raise the old compost level to an inch or so below the rim. Filter more compost round the outside and firm in with the fingers, adding a final ¼-in layer to just cover the old compost. Do not water in.

On completion, replace the label and insert a 12-in length of split bamboo (called a "flower stick") positioned close to the stem, having sharpened the stake at one end to facilitate easy penetration and prevent root damage. Tie loosely with soft garden twine, taking the tying material round the plant stem and stake in a figure of eight, continuing with a second loop round the stake.

Stock Selection

In many cases plants of a particular variety will be equal in vigour and healthy, but there are cases where plants do not grow on completely satisfactorily in first pots and foliage can become chlorotic with the plant obviously suffering from some defect. Again, it is advisable at all stages to carry a few spares and to select the best for potting on, plus at this stage one or two spares of each variety for final selection at planting out or final potting.

Keep Close For A Few Days

After potting, stand plants back in the frame and keep them close for a day or two, then revert to normal ventilation. Recommence watering when they have obviously reached the point of need.

Don't Overcrowd

Second pots may stand close together at first, but in a very short time respacing will be necessary. Avoid overcrowding. Plants must have light and air if weak, drawn growth is to be avoided. Continue spacing as development proceeds.

Bedded Plants

Where plants have been bedded direct into the frames the grower is spared the demands of this phase, but he should at least provide bamboo flower stakes if stems lengthen unduly.

CHAPTER 7

Stopping and Timing

The Natural Sequence

Allowed to develop in its own way, a chrysanthemum continues to lengthen its main stem for some weeks, then begins to produce small sidegrowths in its leaf axils. Soon afterwards a flower bud appears in the tip. This "break bud", as it is termed, terminates the lengthening of the main stem and completely diverts the energy of the plant into the sidegrowths (also referred to as "breaks" or "laterals"). The sidegrowths, in fact, commandeer the sap flow to such an extent that the break bud becomes starved and withers. It develops into a flower only if the young laterals are promptly removed.

The development of each of the newly formed laterals proceeds in exactly the same way as the main stem, with a flower bud (this time called a "first crown bud") eventually forming in each tip and a new crop of laterals (or secondary flower buds) emerging from the leaf axils. (The appearance of multiple flower buds, whether at this point or at a later stage, marks the end of vegetative development. They are thus referred to as "terminal buds".)

In most cases, however, where a plant is allowed to grow naturally a third system of laterals emerge from the leaf axils below the central second crown bud, and these grow on to produce the terminal buds (in this case "third crown buds") in the shoot tips and leaf axils.

Left to its own devices a plant flowers on its terminal buds – there being no further laterals to continue vegetative growth – whether they be first, second or third crown (see Fig. 7.1).

What Is Stopping?

Stopping is no more than the removal of the tiny growing tip to channel vigour into developing laterals earlier than would have been the case had the plant been allowed to develop naturally. But the timing of the stop and the reasons for stopping are important.

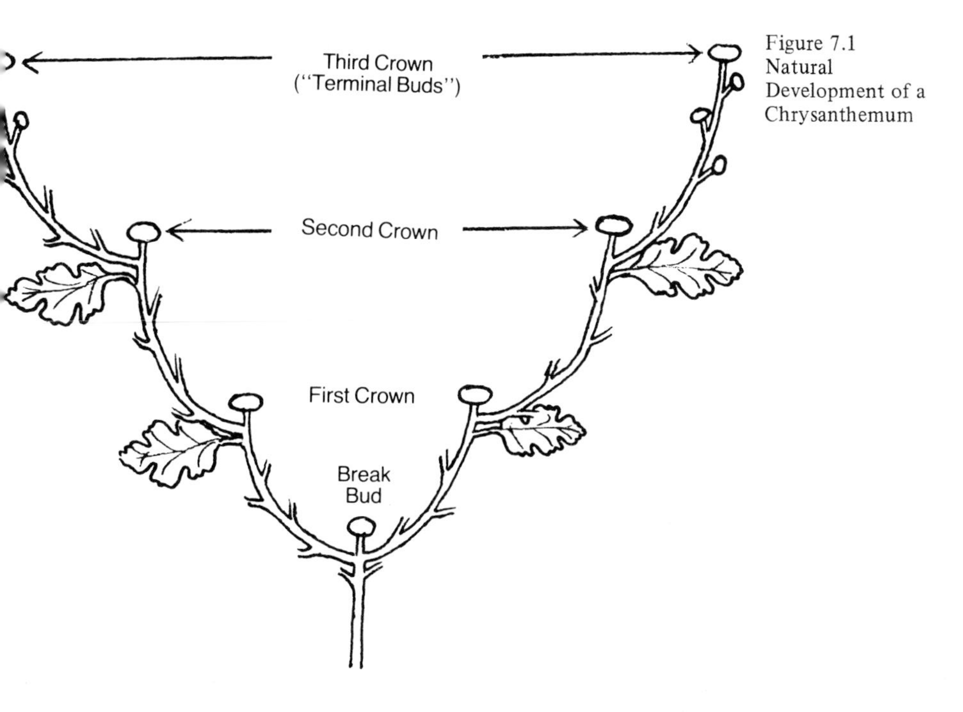

Figure 7.1
Natural
Development of a
Chrysanthemum

The "terminal bud" will be surrounded by other flower buds and marks the end of vegetative development. It is most likely to occur on third crown, though it may be on second or even first crown.

We Must Aim At A Full Leaf Count

In considering stopping we should again reflect on the dry weight theory and on the fact that long, strong laterals are needed for full-sized blooms. As we saw, to have any chance of producing full-sized blooms it is essential to have full-sized laterals, which means that they must develop strongly with a full quota of leaves before the flower buds appear in their tips, for only if laterals produce their full quota of leaves which gradually increase in size as they ascend the stem can they be the longest, strongest possible laterals for the variety with full size potential.

Varieties vary in the maximum number of leaves they normally produce before flower buds are initiated. One variety may produce flower buds after, say, 36 leaves have developed on its laterals while another may not produce its buds until 50 leaves have formed. The former will have maximum size potential at 36 leaves and the latter at 50 leaves. So we need 36 leaves gradually increasing in size in the first instance and 50 in the latter. The value of a full leaf count will be lost where successive leaves do not gradually increase in size.

Flower buds may appear in lateral tips before the full quota of leaves have developed, however, (a) due to rising temperatures (more especially rising night temperatures), (b) due to shortening days – or rather longer nights, or (c) as a result of a combination of these two factors.

Earlies are especially sensitive to the effect of rising temperatures in inducing bud initiation, and as a result when summer temperatures rise they tend to initiate buds, the tendency increasing as more leaves develop. This means that earlies will normally initiate buds in late June or early July irrespective of how many leaves they have developed. If the full leaf count has been reached, or nearly reached, this is of no consequence, for we shall have full-sized laterals with every chance of their carrying full-sized blooms. But where the leaf count is considerably reduced due to a late stop followed by relatively quick bud initiation (as a result of rising temperatures) we shall have short laterals of reduced bloom-size potential. The answer is simple. Earlies must be rooted and stopped sufficiently early in the season to ensure that they develop a full leaf count, or nearly so, before temperatures become so high that buds are initiated.

The stop will need to be earlier for some varieties than others, depending on how quickly they develop their full leaf count, and this will vary from locality to locality, even in different gardens and under different cultural conditions. Plants growing vigorously in a well-aerated soil or compost will tend to develop their full leaf count more quickly than those growing slowly in a more solid medium, and those in warm gardens will tend to initiate buds earlier than those in cold gardens. Both factors can influence personal stopping dates for a particular variety.

Stop Earlies By Mid-May

As established growers of earlies will know, stops applied in June in an endeavour to produce later blooms often lead to small blooms developing on short laterals with a limited leaf count, whereas blooms developing on plants of the same variety stopped by mid-May are usually much larger, on long laterals, and, due to their extra substance and extra petallage do not mature much earlier than those stopped later.

For these reasons it is preferable to stop all earlies by mid-May. Some earlies are of course normally stopped before mid-May, since their natural time of flowering is toward the end of September or early October and an early stop is applied to bring flowering forward, which automatically leads to a full leaf count and "natural" bud initiation before temperature has any effect.

In the interests of full bloom size it is preferable to endeavour to bring flowering forward by early stops than to try to delay flowering by later stops. Varieties chosen for late September shows should consist of those which tend to flower naturally in late September and which automatically qualify for an early stop. It is futile to endeavour to flower early September varieties in late September by delaying the stop until the middle of June.

Lates May Be Stopped Later

Lates are less influenced by temperature, though they tend to flower earlier in warm seasons than in cool seasons. They continue to grow vegetatively until (a) the plant has developed its full leaf count on its laterals, or (b) daylength is sufficiently reduced to cause the development of flower-inducing hormones, which are synthesised in the leaves and translocated to the growing tips of the laterals to induce flower bud initiation.

Generally speaking, daylength needs to be reduced to approximately 14½ hours before buds are initiated, and 13½ hours before they further develop as embryo flowers. This means that in southern Britain buds will not normally be initiated due to shortening days until the second half of August. It will be a little later further north. Most lates are grown by amateurs to flower in late October or the first half of November. This means that in the majority of cases stops will be applied sufficiently early for laterals to have developed their full quota of leaves and for buds to have been initiated before bud-initiating effects of reducing daylength become effective.

So lates will automatically develop their full complement of leaves on their laterals under standard cultural routines with full bloom-size potential. The exception is where bud initiation needs to be delayed until toward the end of August or into September, a situation which will apply to few varieties, except perhaps late flowering singles, and here a reduction in leaf count will not be as crucial as with double-flowered blooms of greater substance.

Stop When In Stopping Condition

We suggested in discussing propagation that cuttings should be inserted in twelve to sixteen weeks ahead of the stopping date in order to have plants in "stopping condition" on the stopping date. This is important. It is not sufficient to produce just a percentage of full-sized blooms: *all* our blooms need to be of full size, which means that all our laterals need to be full sized, and this can be assured by the stopping technique.

In the weeks immediately following rooting, growth buds in the leaf axils are virtually dormant, but as the stem lengthens and successive leaves develop, growth buds in their axils show an increasing tendency to active development. The higher up the stem they are, the more active they become. If a plant is stopped before growth buds have become active they will be slow to develop, and in many cases the topmost lateral will eventually grow away strongly, with one or two weaker laterals below. As we have seen, the bloom is relative to the lateral which bears it, and therefore in such cases we shall have blooms of different sizes and different qualities, while our aim must be to have all the blooms of a particular variety of similar full size and quality.

Figure 7.2
Plant not yet in Stopping Condition

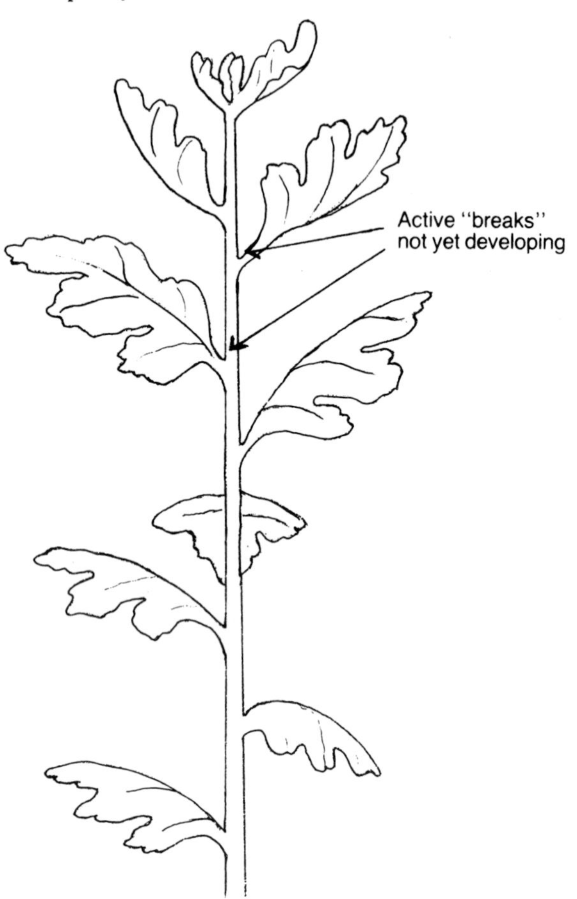

But if the plants are rooted sufficiently early to ensure that they have reached the stage where they are producing *active* embryo laterals in their leaf axils by the stopping date and then only the tiny growing tip of the main stem is removed, say a ¼ in, the upper growth buds will develop strongly and evenly, giving a crop of four or five laterals of equal vigour closely grouped at the top of the main stem, and ensuring an even crop of blooms.

Furthermore, a plant stopped after it is in stopping condition will grow on without check, and with the plant continuing to develop

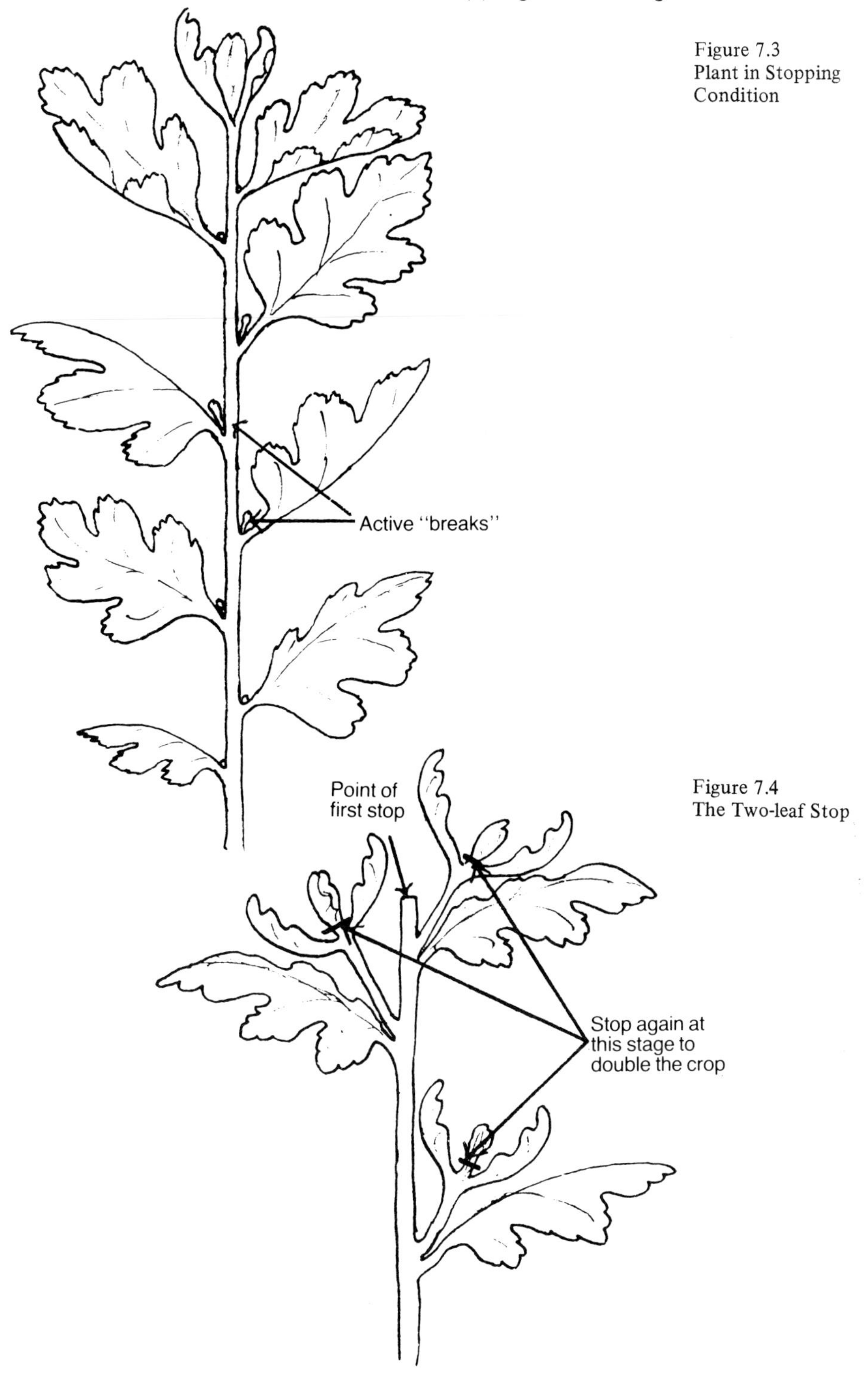

Figure 7.3
Plant in Stopping Condition

Figure 7.4
The Two-leaf Stop

healthily, whereas a plant stopped before it is in stopping condition is bound to check, for its growth momentum will have been suddenly disrupted. Where stops are applied too soon lower leaves can become discoloured and wither, and the state of check can be so severe as to have an adverse effect on the healthy development of the plant for the remainder of the season, with a consequent reduction in bloom quality.

The "Two-Leaf" Stop

Where too few laterals emerge we can apply what is referred to as a "two-leaf" stop with a view to doubling the crop. The first two leaves and laterals emerge as an almost opposite pair, and if the growing tip of the new lateral is nipped out as soon as the first pair of leaves have formed, two new "breaks" will emerge from the two leaf axils to produce blooms which are little delayed and of good quality.

"Natural Breaks"

In some cases late-flowering varieties are grown on a "natural break". In other words the flower bud appears in the tip of the main stem and a stop as such is not applied. Laterals will subsequently develop from the leaf axils of the main stem, but it is as well to remove those closest to the bud and to run on for flowering purposes a set of laterals several inches lower down the stem; this ensures no possibility of the flowering impulse having spread into the laterals to lead to premature budding before the full leaf quota has developed.

Timing

Timing is the art of producing blooms on a predetermined date. Its practice in the amateur ranks is more the concern of exhibitors and those desirous of producing flowers for Christmas or special functions.

Chrysanthemums flower early or late depending on the inherent characteristics of each variety, but the actual dates can be varied by such things as (a) the latitude and aspect of the plot on which they are grown, (b) the weather, (c) cultural methods, and (d) the rooting and stopping procedure. Some flower naturally as early as July; others not until October and November.

Latitude, plot situation and weather are beyond control, but some degree of adjustment can be made by varying stopping and rooting dates.

Timing Begins With The Production Of Cuttings

Practised intensively, timing begins with the trimming of stools, the aim being to produce basal growths of suitable length by the date of rooting.

Cuttings should then be inserted on a date calculated to produce plants in stopping condition on the stopping date, that is 16 weeks ahead of the stop for cuttings inserted by mid-January, 14 weeks for cuttings inserted between mid-January and mid-February and 12 weeks in advance for later batches. These are general guidelines. A season's trial will indicate where adjustment is needed for particular varieties.

There is a limit to the adjustment of flowering dates, but to advance flowering we must root and stop earlier, which will have the effect of plants developing their full leaf quota and initiating buds earlier. On average, flowering is only a half to one-third earlier than any advance made to the stopping date. Early buds tend to "hold" somewhat, but as a result they tend to produce larger flowers with more florets, so long as the full leaf quota has been achieved. Some varieties run up a long "neck" under the bud when the buds appear early (in long days) for the variety, whereas later buds of the same variety will develop with leaves close to the bud.

Delayed flowering can be achieved by rooting and stopping later – less practicable with temperature-sensitive earlies than with lates – or they can be stopped a second time to produce "second crown" blooms, by stopping the first laterals to produce a second lateral crop. This technique is seldom applied to earlies, but it is commonly used for some of the earlier flowered large exhibition varieties, for late-flowering incurves and singles. Where buds appear early after only one stop the resultant blooms usually contain more florets than where buds appear later as a result of a second stop; this can be an important bloom quality consideration for the exhibitor, especially with incurves where a nicely closed top is desirable, and with singles with their need of a clear, floret-free central disc.

Bud Timing

Some varieties develop buds within a month of the final stop, some take as long as ten weeks, or even longer. Buds of September-flowering earlies are generally secured in July, early in the month for early September flowers and late in the month for late September. In the case of late-flowering varieties, most large exhibition buds are secured in the first half of August; incurves, reflexes and intermediates in the second half of August or early September, and singles from late August to mid-September.

Even where careful records are kept and cultivation follows a well-established routine, seasons can so vary that bud and bloom dates are either advanced or delayed. Little can be done to hasten the development of buds forming later than desired, save prompt disbudding, but where buds appear early bloom maturity can be delayed by a few days by allowing sidegrowths close under the bud to develop to several inches in length before removing them. However, there is always the likelihood of reducing bloom size, and in some cases tiny buds become "blind" and fail to develop if sidegrowths are retained for too long.

Another point to bear in mind and one which leads to different timings with growers using the same stopping dates is that laterals develop to bud initiation more quickly in soilless composts and open soils than in more solid composts and soils. Similarly, plants in small pots or on a low diet are less free in lateral development than the same varieties in large pots or on a more generous diet, and plants in "cold gardens" tend to bloom later (with more leaves on their laterals) than in "warm gardens", though the affect varies with the variety.

The "Run-by"

It sometimes happens that buds appear several weeks before they are required, and obviously flowering will be far too early. The answer here is to resort to a "run-by", i.e. to remove the flower buds and "run on" the lateral next under each bud. This is in effect a natural second stop, and the result will be blooms of second crown characteristics flowering several weeks later, the extent of the delay varying with the variety. If the operation is carried out promptly and a shoot close to the bud is selected the new stem will continue as a straight extension of the original.

Buds To Colour; Colour To Full Bloom

The time taken from the securing of buds to colour show, and from colour show to full bloom is also variable, but it is generally more predictable than the period from the stop to bud appearance and securing. Small-flowered and medium-flowered blooms mature more quickly than large-flowered; similarly, most reflexes and intermediates tend to mature more quickly than incurves which need to develop all their florets to reach their peak of perfection. In the majority of cases the period between bud selection and colour show is approximately four weeks. Between colour show and full bloom it is a little over three weeks for smaller reflexes and intermediates, and a few days more for incurves, with another week for larger blooms. Large exhibition blooms develop over a longer period, up to six weeks in some cases, but singles will mature in three weeks or so from colour show.

"Holding" blooms

Blooms likely to be just "over the top" by show day may be held in condition for a few days longer by cutting them several days in advance of normal and keeping them in a cool, airy but light room. Commercial growers resort to refrigeration. Conversely, warm storage conditions will encourage more speedy development.

Where bloom timing is an important consideration we suggest that the grower makes his assessments for each variety in reverse order, working back from the desired date of bloom maturity, through colour show, bud selection, stopping, and cuttings insertion to the trimming of stools for cuttings production. Then after assessments have been made a varietal list should be prepared in date sequence, for each of the phases. These will be helpful as references as the season progresses.

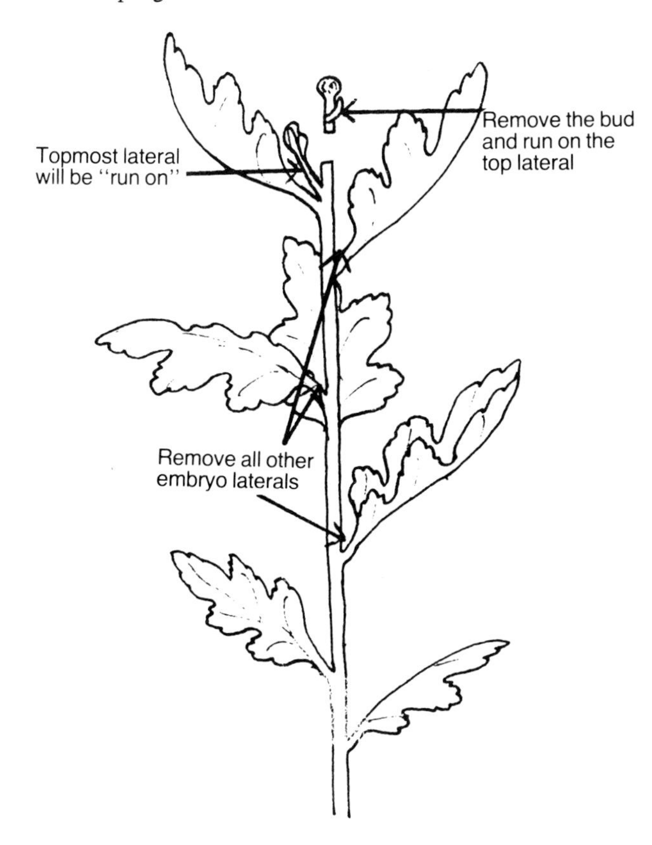

Figure 7.5
The "Run-by"

CHAPTER 8

Planting the Earlies

The planting of earlies should take place as soon as the risk of sharp frosts has passed. Mid-May is a suitable period in the southern part of Britain, but planting may need to be delayed for a week or more in the north.

Where a whole plot is to be devoted to early chrysanthemums make out a plan in advance, arranging varieties according to height. The plot should have been deeply forked and the soil broken into a tilth some weeks before; a base dressing of a fertiliser equally balanced in nitrogen, phosphorus and potassium should have been raked into the surface layers at approximately 4 oz per square yard. This will help to ensure that the plants get away to a good start and grow on strongly. In contrast with earlier teaching, we believe that most soils should not be consolidated by treading or rolling prior to planting, but should be left loosely forked and raked to ensure the necessary aeration for healthy root development.

When planning the planting programme look ahead to the plant development and blooming period and arrange for all plants to be reasonably accessible. With these requirements in mind it is best to plan on the basis of two-row beds with a 30 in gangway between each bed. Three-row beds are the maximum. Rows should be 18 in apart with canes inserted 18 in apart in the rows. The very closest spacing would be 15 in between rows and 15 in between plants; 4 ft canes are regarded as generally most suitable, and they should be pressed into the soil to a depth of about 9 in. A small plumb-bob on a 3 ft cord is useful when inserting the canes, since it ensures that they are vertical and at a uniform height. Nothing looks worse than canes inserted at sundry heights and different angles.

Plant When The Soil Is Friable

Planting is best carried out when the soil is friable, i.e. crumbly. If it is wet and soggy delay planting for a few days.

Water plants some hours before planting, then take out the holes with a trowel. Set the plants as close to their canes as practicable and to the same level as the old compost ball. Pack the soil gently round the roots with the butt of the trowel and level off. Tie the plants loosely to their canes with a figure-of-eight. Insert labels, clear away pots and make the plot tidy as you proceed. The planting operation is no more complicated than this.

Figure 8.1 Planting out an Early

Plants from frame beds should be similarly watered some hours before planting, and they should be lifted with as little root disturbance as possible. Root spread will be more extensive than where plants have been grown in pots and the holes made to receive them will need to be larger. Otherwise, the planting routine is the same.

This is another occasion when stock selection should be practised. Where spares are held plants should be selected carefully, discarding any that are weak or exhibiting suspicious foliar symptoms.

Anti-Bird Precautions

Unfortunately, many gardeners have sparrow problems, one of their spring delicacies being young chrysanthemum leaves. Back-garden chrysanthemums can be severely damaged and shoot tips removed in the first weeks after planting. The attacks usually stop about midsummer, but this is too late if the necessary precautions have not already been taken. Strips of silver foil suspended from canes act as a temporary deterrent, but the most effective remedy is undoubtedly strands of black cotton criss-crossed on canes around and over each block when planting is complete. This should be regarded as an automatic part of the planting routine.

Plants In Borders

Where gardeners plant sprays or disbuds in mixed borders, preparation, planting and precautions against sparrows should be exactly the same, but if the requirement is a massed display of sprays in the autumn the planting distance could be reduced to a foot each way.

CHAPTER 9

Final Pots for Lates

While early flowering chrysanthemums are planted into the open garden, greenhouse types develop in large pots (referred to as "finals"), standing outside in the summer months and being transferred to the greenhouse for flowering to prevent damage by late autumn frosts, wind and rain. In fact, in earlier times pot-grown chrysanthemums had a respected place in the annual cycle of plants to be seen in the large greenhouses on the estates of landed gentry, and their head gardeners used closely guarded and "secret" methods for their cultivation. Fortunately, there are few secrets today, and results are at best very near to perfection.

When To Pot

Plants are ready for final potting between early May and the end of June, depending on the date of rooting and the root vigour of the variety. An average period is five weeks after potting into second pots. Large exhibition and other early rooted types are usually ready first. The extent of root development is the deciding factor. As with the previous potting, roots should be well in evidence round the outside of the old compost ball and should be encircling the base before repotting is undertaken. The operation may spread over several weeks, small numbers (or dozens where large collections are concerned) being potted as they become ready. Plants should not be potted on as a batch irrespective of root development.

Assemble Materials In Advance

Materials should again be assembled well in advance. Pots should be sterilised and dry, the compost should be in a correctly moist condition and large and small crocks (broken pieces of clay pots) should be on hand to provide for drainage.

Though there are still many pet recipes for final composts for chrysanthemums, we have found nothing to beat properly prepared John Innes No. 3 – though excellent results can be enjoyed from the more recent soilless composts. A bushel of compost will pot approximately ten plants from 5 in into 8½ in pots, eight into 9 in pots, and six into 10 in pots, with a hundredweight potting half as many again.

Pot Sizes

Pot sizes are almost as controversial as composts. There is one generally accepted principle, however: strong-rooted varieties need a larger pot than those with a weak root system. The amount of top growth is not always a good guide to the size of the pot needed. Some dwarf varieties have strong root systems and need a larger pot than taller varieties with a weak root system. A good indication of root vigour can be obtained when plants are knocked from their 5 in pots.

There is a tendency to put incurves into small pots to restrict growth, and produce smaller but tighter blooms, but the use of open soilless composts with their open construction has completely disproved the need. Blooms of incurves grown in large pots of open soilless compost are larger, while retaining the desired form. The normal minimum size should be considered 8½ in, but these should be used for only very delicate rooted varieties. Most need a 9 in or 10 in, irrespective of their bloom type. Incidentally, final pots should be measured at their inside diameter an inch below the rim.

Pot Carefully And Systematically

Potting is again a simple operation, but it should be carried out thoughtfully, and if it is undertaken steadily and systematically it can be one of the most satisfying operations in the chrysanthemum year – and so much depends on it!

Place one large crock concave-side-downward over the drainage hole and overlay with an inch or so of medium crocks. Cover these with an inch of fibrous peat. This should be sufficient to ensure good drainage. Add 2 or 3 in of compost and firm gently with the blunt end of a pot rammer. The pot rammer can be conveniently made from an old chairleg approximately 2 in in diameter, but shaped to an oval at one end. Remove the plant from its pot (having watered it some hours before), remove any withered or yellow lower leaves, and then stand centrally on the layer of compost. Add further compost round the outside of the old compost ball and firm in lightly with the oval end of the pot rammer in such a way that roots are not damaged. Add further compost and complete with a ¼ in or so over the old compost ball. The finished level should be in the region of 2 in below the pot rim to allow for watering and later top dressings. Insert the label and stand potthick in a sheltered position. It is not necessary to insert canes at this stage where plants have already been provided with a split bamboo flower stick.

This is again an important time for stock selection, and any doubtful plants should be finally discarded.

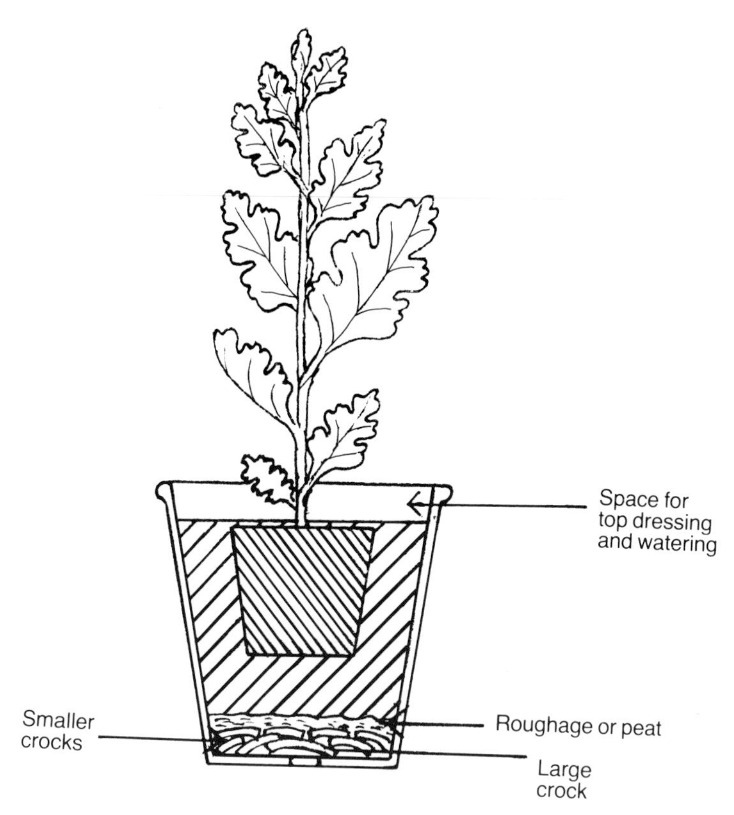

Figure 9.1
Final Potting

Earlier generations of chrysanthemum growers indulged in very firm ramming, and one hears of instances where pots were – boastfully – broken in the process. The extent to which ramming is desirable – or permissible – depends on the constitution of the material being rammed. When quality turf-loam, very spongy in texture, was available and much used, firm ramming was acceptable since the compost remained aerated, but we have seen seasons ruined where ramming of more solid mediums had been excessive. Once again, roots must be able to "breathe"! Final potting must be properly carried out or the season will be a failure.

Our recommended alternative to John Innes composts are the very "open" soilless composts based on pure peat or peat and sand. Where these are employed the originators advise that they be no more than firmed gently with the fingers! And there is nothing wrong with the blooms produced in them. In fact, in recent years many of the trophy and best-in-show winners at the National shows in London have been grown in soilless composts. So there can be little wrong with open mediums.

Ideally, plants will not need watering for a week to ten days after final potting, and in dull seasons this may be practicable, but so often sunshine will have them drying out and flagging badly within a few days. Mild flagging with plants freshening overnight is of no concern, but when leaves hang limply down the stem a drink is obviously needed. For the first two weeks any watering is best applied as far as possible in the region of the old soil ball, applying, say, half a pint to each plant. This will keep them reasonably fresh while encouraging the roots to penetrate the new compost. At the end of the fortnight water can be given more generously, say the equivalent of a level inch all over the pot (about a pint and a half) whenever a plant is in need. But water must never be given where the compost ball is still moist.

On To The Standing Ground

This is the moment to transfer plants to their summer quarters, the "standing ground". By this time they should be nicely settled in their pots and well able to stand up to more airy conditions.

The standing ground should, for preference, be in an open position well away from tall buildings, but ideally with some form of natural screen on the side of the prevailing wind. As an alternative a screen of runner beans is helpful. A well-drained pest-free base should be provided (a) to ensure good drainage from the pots, and (b) to enable cultural operations to be carried out cleanly and pleasantly under all weather conditions. Some growers stand their pots on concrete or paving slabs, and some on boards, but with flat surfaces there is always a risk of a seal forming between the pot and the base, preventing good drainage – and good drainage is vital! A satisfactory alternative, and one which answers all requirements, is to cover the area of the standing ground with a 2-in layer of coarse shingle. This provides for good drainage and is always clean to walk on.

Now is the time to insert a cane or canes to each pot. Where large exhibition plants are concerned one cane inserted centrally will be sufficient, but where a crop of several blooms is to be carried two canes should be inserted. Stout 4-ft canes are sufficient in most cases, but where a variety is known to be tall they may need to be 5 or even 6 ft.

Pots should stand 18 in apart in rows 18 in apart, with ideally a gangway 2 ft 6 in to 3 ft wide between each two-row block. Where space is plentiful, dedicated growers go further and have single rows with gangways in between.

In order to prevent damage in strong winds, posts and straining wires must be provided, a post being driven into the ground at the end of each row with intermediate posts at intervals of nine to twelve feet. A "straining wire" should be stretched tautly between the posts at about 3 ft 9 in above the ground. Satisfactory straining wires may be made from old plastic-covered electric cable. Tie each cane, or clip it with a wire clip, to the wire in such a way that it cannot move sideways in strong winds.

Sparrows can still be troublesome and our practice is therefore to run a strand of black cotton between the canes several inches above the straining wire to prevent sparrows using it as a perch. This tends to scare them and keep them away. If, in spite of black cotton, sparrows do prove troublesome, metal-foil bird scarers suspended from the straining wires at intervals help to deter them.

One final task. In the interests of even moisture penetration we make a point of levelling each pot with a spirit level; this is readily achieved on a shingle base.

CHAPTER 10

The Growing Season

The steady progress of plants in the weeks following planting out and final potting is important, for any serious check to growth will be reflected in the season's results. By thoughtful preparation of the soil for earlies and of the compost for lates we shall have put in sound foundations, but there are points to watch and things to do on a daily and weekly basis, bearing in mind the need of long, strong laterals.

If the season is wet and the soil keeps moist, earlies will become established and keep moving forward without assistance, but in dry seasons they may soon be flagging, with leaves hanging limply down the stem. Some growers seem to relish such a situation, declaring that this will make the roots "search for moisture". A soggy soil may be unhealthy, but parched plants will not be growing during the period of severe wilting, and if they have not refreshed overnight they must be given water. Short periods of mild flagging at this stage may do no harm, but it is wrong to leave plants in distress for a week or more, as sometimes advocated, and lose a period of lateral development. The same principles apply to lates in pots. If in the early weeks after potting plants are flagging and fail to freshen overnight they must be watered.

Daily And Weekly Rounds

In fact, any self-respecting chrysanthemum enthusiast will inspect his plants each day, and an early morning round to cover water and other minor needs should become part of a satisfying routine; it also keeps one in key with one's plants. A walk up and down the rows and a glance at each plant and shoot tip will ensure that nothing gets out of hand. You may find signs of aphids building up in "muggy" spells; the small leaves of a shoot tip may be folded over and webbed together by the tiny tortrix moth caterpillar – the leaves should be gently unfolded with the tip of a penknife blade and the caterpillar despatched, otherwise the lateral will be ruined; the odd earwig found in a shoot tip can be deftly removed with tweezers; or you may catch a green or brown capsid bug moving quickly into hiding behind an upper stem. When pests are found it will put you on your guard and you must make a special point of countering them with an appropriate insecticide.

A more thorough weekly inspection should be made of every plant for purposes of tying, for the removal of unwanted growths and for a more thorough inspection for pests and diseases. While it is sometimes suggested that one should spray only when pests are observed, we advise a routine spray with a general-purpose insecticide on completion of each weekly round. This will account for aphids, caterpillars and the insidious leaf miner, which can cause so much damage and disfigure leaves if regular spraying is not carried out. Fungicides are not usually needed early in the season, but as August approaches mildew is likely to put in an appearance, and from the first signs of the disease a mildew specific should be added to the routine spray every two weeks.

In recent times white rust has caused concern among commercial chrysanthemum growers and there is a possibility that it could spread into amateur collections by way of imported plants. White rust produces small white pustules on the undersides of leaves, as distinct from the smooth white downy effect of mildew and the white serpentine trails of leaf miner grubs. It is a notifiable disease in Britain, and wherever an outbreak is suspected your county horticultural authority should be notified immediately.

Lateral Countdown To Crop, Plus One Spare

Where plants were in stopping condition at the time of stopping, they should produce a crop of strong young laterals from their leaf axils, the number varying with the variety. Some produce only a few, while others produce many. There is no point in retaining a forest of unwanted growths and the excess should be removed by the time they are 2 or 3 in long, in order to channel the full vigour of the plant into the crop to be carried. Large exhibition plants are normally flowered at only one bloom to the plant, but it is advisable to retain two laterals up to bud appearance. If only one is carried and its tip is damaged a whole season is lost. The second lateral offsets the risk, and by counting down to one at bud appearance a brief period of extra, and desirable, vigour is provided for in the remaining bud. Large-flowered earlies are normally cropped at two blooms to the plant, with mediums at three and small at four; late-flowering incurves, reflexes and intermediates normally carry similar crops. Singles are usually flowered at four to six blooms in the case of large-flowered, and between six and ten for mediums. So it is down to crop plus one spare as soon as practicable, with a view to removing the spare at bud selection.

Remove Sideshoots And Basal Growths

As laterals lengthen, some varieties will soon begin to develop small growths in their leaf axils and these must be removed. Remove them just as soon as they are big enough to handle. Later, when secondary flower buds and/or shoots develop around the central flower bud it will be necessary to remove them also. The aim with disbudded varieties is to finally have laterals with just the central bud retained at the tip, with all sideshoots removed from the leaf axils. But early flowering sprays carry four to six laterals, with no disbudding, except where special balance in the spray is required for purposes of exhibition. Late-flowering sprays can be stopped to produce three laterals, or they can be "flowered straight up" on the main stem (see Chapter 15).

Figure 10.1 Lateral in Need of Disbudding and Deshooting and Lateral Disbudded and Deshooted

Some varieties begin to produce small basal growths through the soil quite early in the season. As mentioned previously, these should be nipped back to soil level on the weekly round. As lower stems harden, bottom leaves will in many cases begin to yellow and wither. While they should be removed, this should occasion no concern unless the yellowing and withering becomes rampant and spreads rapidly up the plant, in which case it could be caused by verticillium wilt or eelworm. If in doubt seek knowledgeable local advice.

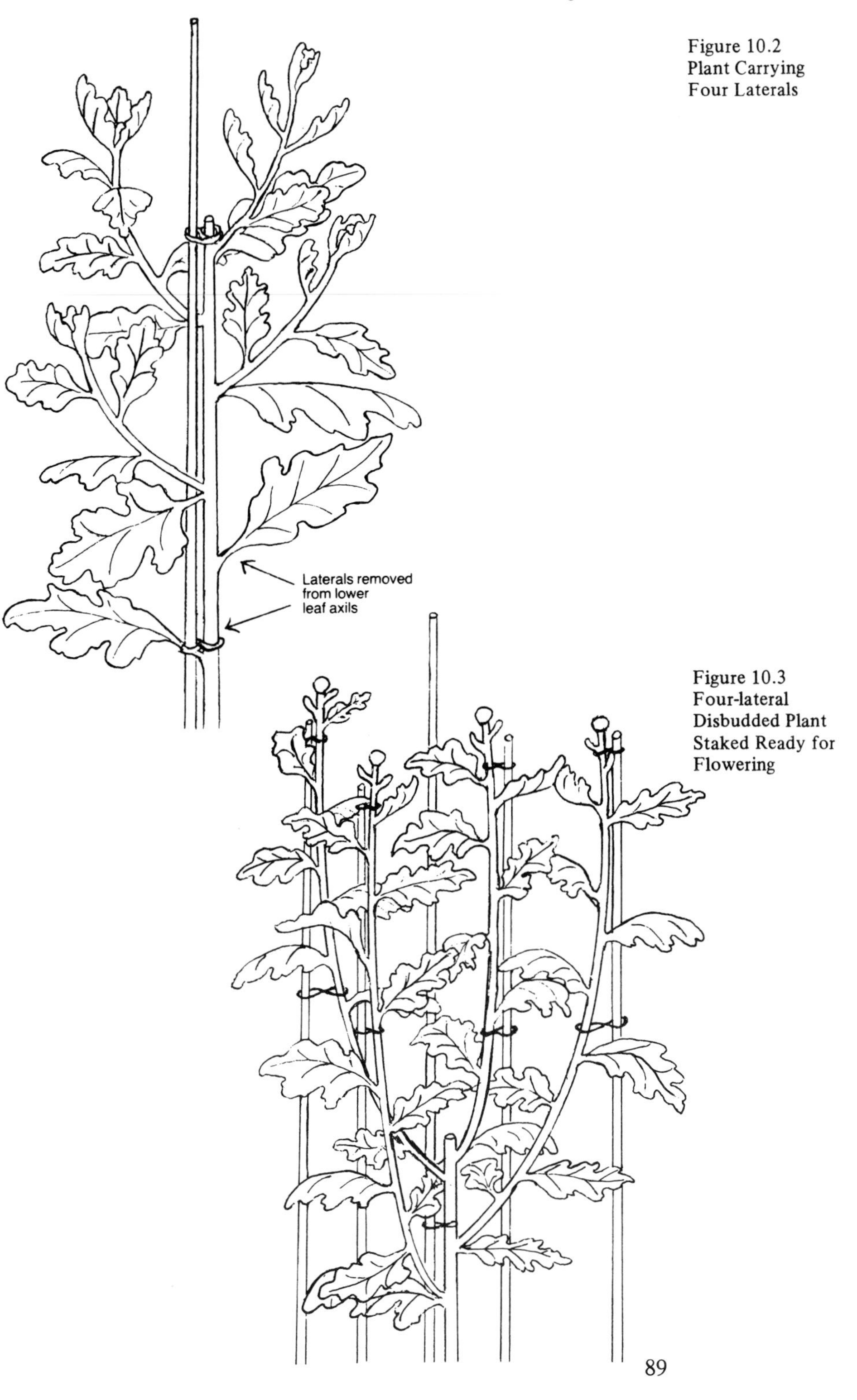

Figure 10.2
Plant Carrying
Four Laterals

Figure 10.3
Four-lateral
Disbudded Plant
Staked Ready for
Flowering

The Watering Routine

Watering is sufficiently important to justify further consideration, but at the same time it must be kept in perspective as a straightforward cultural operation rather than an intricate art.

While mild flagging may do little harm, a plant must enjoy a constant and adequate water supply from the time of rooting to bloom maturity. It should be borne in mind that during periods of flagging a plant will not be photosynthesising, i.e. producing growth materials in its leaves (by day), or extending its tissues. At the other extreme where roots are virtually standing in water the oxygen content of the soil or compost will be so reduced as to impair root functions, and where lengthy periods of waterlogging are experienced roots will be in danger of destruction by what amounts to drowning – they need oxygen for respiration in exactly the same way as animals and humans.

In practical terms, sufficient water should be applied to moisten the soil or compost thoroughly whenever a plant reaches the point of flagging, or just before this point is reached; then it should be left until the point of need is again reached. Such tactics will ensure that the full water needs of the plant are met, and in properly prepared soils and composts the oxygen requirements of roots will also be adequately catered for.

Earlies should be watered whenever the surface layers have dried, at, say, two gallons to the square yard. In hot weather watering may be needed twice a week, but there are usually dull, wet periods during the season when plants can go for weeks without assistance. Lates in pots must be inspected for water needs at least daily, and only those in need or reaching the point of need should be watered. Assessments can again be visual, water being given as soon as the surface layers of the compost have dried; or they can be by the pot-tapping technique, pots being tapped in turn with a "pot tapper" – a cotton reel on a bamboo cane. When the compost is drying and receding from the pot walls a clay pot will "ring" when tapped. A dull thud indicates that the compost is still moist. But the tapping method is not satisfactory where pots are cracked, and it cannot be used for plastic pots or soilless composts. Here you will have to water visually and give a thorough soaking as soon as the surface of the compost has dried.

A level inch of water will be sufficient to soak loam composts in final pots, but 2 in will be needed for soilless. The aim is to saturate the entire compost ball without so flooding it that water flows freely from the drainage holes. Soilless composts absorb considerable quantities and they need more than loams – too little can result in the lower levels drying out completely, with roots confined to the upper layers. This is particularly likely where pots have been overfilled with compost and too little space is left at the top.

Feeding Begins

"Feeding!" – a magic word in horticulture, and not least where chrysanthemums are concerned. The key to glorious success, it can also be the cause of failure.

Feeding is normally resorted to in order to increase the rate of growth and the size of the plant, but it can be used to change the condition of growth, and in the case of the chrysanthemum we must bear in mind that we are dealing with a flowering subject and that feeding techniques need to be somewhat different from those employed for leafy vegetables. In the case of exhibition chrysanthemums it is necessary to consider *condition* of growth as well as bulk of growth.

Figure 10.4
"Long-V" Lateral

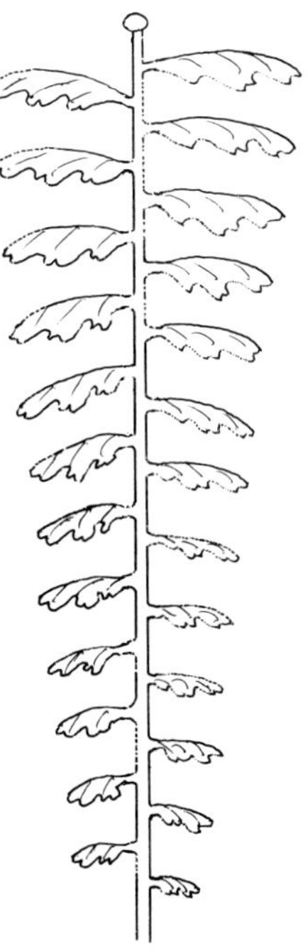

Ideally, successive leaves will become gradually larger from the emergence of the lateral to the bud

The aim must be to have leaves steadily increasing in size as they ascend the stem, so that each lateral appears in the form of a "long-V" when viewed from the side. Vigour in the topmost leaves will further increase when buds appear in the growing tips, and their size and condition are sound indicators of the vigour of development enjoyed in the bud; this will have a profound effect on bloom size and quality. Full leaf count on the laterals will be wasted unless steadily accelerating vigour can be ensured, especially in the topmost leaves. What is in the top leaves will be in the bud.

Some growers restrict feeds to pot plants in the pre-bud period, then feed more heavily during the bud, but there is always the danger that such tactics will throw plants out of "flowering condition" and lead to bloom damping. We favour a continuous and more moderate development with moderate acceleration in the bud.

Where the soil is fertile, properly prepared and well aerated, roots of earlies will continue to spread into untapped areas of nutrition, leaves will gradually enlarge in the desired manner as they ascend the stem and little, if any, feeding should be necessary. It is only where soils are somewhat impoverished – which they should not be – that routine assistance should be needed. Here weekly or fortnightly feeds with a chrysanthemum fertiliser or a general fertiliser reasonably balanced in nitrogen, phosphorus and potassium, and not too nitrogenous, will be beneficial.

Whether grown for cut-flower purposes or for exhibition, lates in pots will need routine feeding to maintain the desired gradual acceleration in growth. John Innes No. 1 compost, a relatively mild preparation, is used for first pots and the more nutritive No. 2 for second pots. A richer blend, No. 3, is used for finals, and this will sustain the plant in steady development until the roots reach the inside of the pot and begin to twine round the outside of the compost ball. Roots will continue to grow – indeed, healthy roots never stop growing – but although nutrient supplies are not completely exhausted they will no longer be available in sufficient quantities to maintain the plant at its desired level of growth. The aim must be to ensure that laterals continue to build up strongly, and this can only be achieved with pot plants by calculated feeding. The principles are similar for soilless composts and feeding will follow a similar pattern, but with a tendency to a little less rather than a little more.

Many different blends of fertiliser are used for feeding chrysanthemums, and growers tend to have pet recipes. In fact many appear to be constantly seeking a magic ingredient which will produce super blooms to order. There is nothing magical or mysterious about feeding chrysanthemums. We must look to the hard facts and operate accordingly.

Non-exhibitors may find it sufficient to obtain a proprietary chrysanthemum fertiliser and to operate strictly in accordance with the manufacturer's instructions. In fact, some prominent growers resort to well-known general-purpose preparations and just follow their prescribed application with excellent results. But those intent on producing blooms of the highest quality from a range of varieties may wish to probe more deeply and understand more of the inner functions and needs of the flowering plant, with a view to employing a more calculated and variable feeding programme. This applies more especially to disbudded pot plants. We shall detail what we believe to be valid principles.

Although some twelve nutrient elements are needed by the plant, feeding programmes are mainly centred on nitrogen, phosphorus and potassium, bearing in mind that nitrogen can be looked upon as the vegetative growth element and phosphorus and potassium as its balancing agents. Many proprietary fertilisers incorporate other elements, but the main concern is with nitrogen, phosphorus and potassium, sometimes referred to as the "golden tripod". If one of the three is drastically reduced the tripod collapses – they must be available in reasonable balance.

Adequate supplies of nitrogen are desirable in that they lead to increased growth and larger leaves; for leaves are not just decorative adornments, but the sugar-producing "factories" responsible for the manufacture of the plant's basic structural and energy-producing materials, and for the materials from which buds and flowers are formed. Leaves with a large surface area are capable of producing more sugars (by photosynthesis in their chlorophyll cells) than smaller leaves of similar composition, and they are therefore more capable of playing their part in the development of strong laterals. We saw under considerations of the dry weight theory that the longer and stronger the laterals the greater the bloom size potential, all other factors being equal, and therefore adequate supplies of nitrogen are essential.

In the region of 90 per cent of a plant's dry weight is, in fact, derived from sugars manufactured by the leaves and only 10 per cent from the nutrients taken in by the roots. When we further consider that a chrysanthemum plant is 75 per cent to 80 per cent water then actual bulk of nutrients in the plant is seen to be very small, and we could look upon them mainly as activators of plant functions, with leaves as the units which in effect manufacture the substance of the plant. It therefore follows that leaves are needed to produce large amounts of sugars, first for the development of the plant and later for export to buds and blooms. While every plant tissue needs materials derived from sugars for its physical construction, every living cell of every tissue – roots, stems, leaves, buds, and finally blooms – also need sugars as the source of energy for its metabolic functions. Thus, reasonable supplies of nitrogen are desirable for purposes of leaf development.

But beyond a certain point increases in nitrogen supply may further increase leaf size yet make them less efficient as sugar producers and exporters. Leaf efficiency can then be restored, however, by balancing nitrogen with phosphorus and potassium: a reasonable *balance* between the three main nutrient elements is necessary. In fact, most feeding programmes provide for this balance.

Beyond a certain dosage, even balanced supplies of nitrogen, phosphorus and potassium are unable to maintain the sugar-manufacturing and exporting efficiency of the leaf, and the composition of the plant then becomes adversely affected in terms of its bloom producing potential. In other words, *balanced* feeding is a must but we can go too far, even with balanced feeding. There is such a thing as overfeeding. Were it not so, producing quality chrysanthemums would be simply a matter of feeding plants heavily – and it is not!

Leaves *manufacture* sugars, by photosynthesis, but they also *consume* sugars, in respiration, and the more heavily fed and the more dark and bloated leaves become the more sugars they consume. But there is a limit to how much sugar they can produce and once this point has been reached any extra feeding increases their sugar consumption without increasing manufacture. Furthermore, toxic levels of nutrients can be reached and interfere with photosynthesis. So, too heavy feeding upsets the balance of the plant and results in reduced sugar export to developing buds and blooms, which is why the growing of chrysanthemums – indeed of any flowering and fruiting crop – depends on more than just giving generous doses of fertilisers.

Experiments with various levels of nutrition to pot plants have provided us with a sound insight into the practical needs of the chrysanthemum, and they have further shown that varieties vary in just how much they can profitably take.

In earlier times the general idea was to feed with a high nitrogen preparation up to the formation of the bud, say, with twice as much nitrogen as phosphorus and potassium. Feeding was then suspended during the early stages of the bud, then levelled off to equal parts of the three nutrients during bud development. This tended to produce strong laterals, but reduced growth impetus during bud swell, and therefore produced smaller blooms. More recently outlooks have changed and many growers now prefer to build up their laterals with a preparation equally balanced in nitrogen, phosphorus and potassium, switching without pause to a more nitrogenous balance, say, with 50 per cent more nitrogen than phosphorus and potassium, through bud swell to ensure full movement in the bud. The result is that blooms are larger, while still retaining good colour and freshness.

If in the pre-bud period a powder fertiliser with 5 per cent nitrogen, 5 per cent phosphorus and 5 per cent potassium is applied, a sound basic routine would be to feed at a level teaspoon per plant per week, commencing five weeks after final potting until buds appear in the growing tips. If you prefer liquid feeds then mix a preparation containing 10 per cent nitrogen, 10 per cent phosphorus and 10 per cent potassium at a level tablespoon per gallon; a pint of this solution applied to each plant would have an effect similar to the powder. Generally speaking, powder materials are less readily available to the roots than liquids, but they begin to take effect within a few days of application and to be effective over a longer period. A word of warning: plants should always be moist at the roots when fed, otherwise root damage may occur. Powders should always be lightly watered in.

Experience shows that the above diet is sufficient for most types of chrysanthemum and for most varieties. Few need more and some are better with less. Strong-growing varieties tend to "take feed" better than those weaker in growth, but this should not be looked upon as a rule of thumb. In the main, satisfactory results will be achieved by simple adherence to the pattern outlined here, followed by a similar standard routine during bud swell, but there are cases where modification is desirable.

"Condition" Must Be Considered

We have already seen that the production of quality chrysanthemums is not just a matter of heavy feeding. Excess feeding with large bloated leaves dark in colour and brittle to the touch may produce plants which look impressive in terms of bulk, but it is most unlikely to result in quality blooms. Though starved plants will never produce full-sized blooms, grossly overfed plants will also produce blooms which are reduced in size, poor in colour and tousled in form. Where growth is excessively vegetative the plant will be inclined toward continued vegetative growth, and even though buds form and florets develop, their needs will not be fully met. This can be analysed as being caused by an associated reduction in sugar supplies from the leaves to buds and blooms – the "carbon-nitrogen ratio" is too low – but there is a possibility that hormones are also involved.

The main guide to the "condition" of a developing plant is its leaves and stems, leaves enlarging and darkening as the feed level is increased. But leaf characteristics vary greatly with the variety. Some have dark leaves on even a moderate diet, while others remain pale in foliage on considerably heavier feeding, and to further complicate matters one variety will be at its best with darker leaves than another. Assessments are therefore relative to the characteristics of the foliage of the particular variety rather than relative to a standard shade of green. Developing leaves in shoot tips are always somewhat pale in colour, but they darken as they mature, and the more heavily they have been fed the darker they become.

So leaf colour is a guide to condition, and discerning growers inspecting plants midway through the season and through bud swell look to such pointers. Leaf shape is an equally valuable indicator. Where plants have been only lightly fed leaves will be more deeply indented than where extra feed has been given, though leaf shape also varies considerably with the variety.

Leaf texture is the third important indicator. Where nutrition is low, mature leaves will be thin and supple, and will readily fold over the fingers, but as the nutrient level increases they will thicken and toughen, until finally under heavy nutrition they become so bloated and brittle that they crack when folded over a finger. While the thin leaf developed on a minimal diet may point to insufficient vigour to produce full-sized blooms, bloated and brittle leaves are also portents of disappointment.

As an approximate guide, mature leaves should be what is loosely referred to as "mid-privet green" in colour, retaining their indentations, and just sufficiently supple to be folded over the finger with the curl of the leaf without cracking. Experienced growers may be seen testing leaves in this way, and not least when assessing other people's blooms. If in doubt reduce the feed level. Nothing can be done with an overfed plant – once it is overfed it will stay overfed and it is ruined for the season, at least in terms of best results. But there is still a chance where a plant has been slightly underfed in the pre-bud phase.

Counter Excessive Height

As we mentioned in Chapter 3, growth retardants are very effective in controlling the height of chrysanthemums. Use these sprays every three weeks on tall varieties during the period of lateral development, and apply the final spray soon after buds appear. Sprays applied late in the bud may further keep height down, but there is a danger that if they are applied too near to the time of bloom opening they may produce streakiness in the blooms of pinks, reds, bronzes and purples.

Thoughtful growers can make good use of growth retardants in other ways: for example, charms can be made more compact, with the result that their hundreds of blooms completely clothe the plant without undesirable gaps.

Figure 10.5
Shoot Tip before Deshooting and Disbudding

Figure 10.6
Bud Swelling after Deshooting and Disbudding

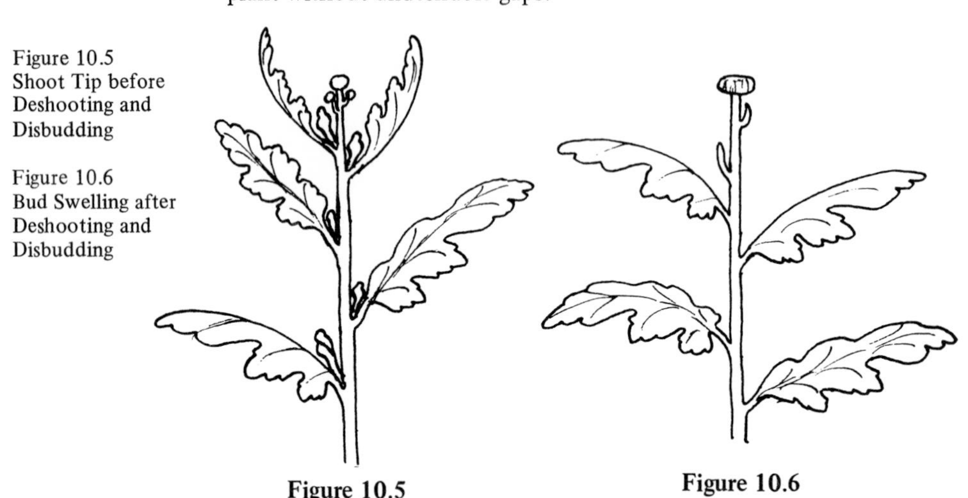

Figure 10.5 Figure 10.6

Bud Initiation

While laterals are continuing in vegetative development, embryo leaves are initiated at set intervals on the tissues behind the tiny extending tip deep inside the cluster of small leaves at the top of the lateral. But when the time comes for flower bud initiation the tiny growing tip begins to flatten to form the "receptacle", or central dome of the bud on which the florets will form. Logically, one can expect that a vigorously growing lateral will produce a sizeable receptacle, whereas a weaker lateral would be expected to produce a small receptacle, and this is a valid outlook. Then one can reflect on the fact that a receptacle will become completely covered with closely packed florets, and therefore the more vigorous the lateral and the larger the receptacle the greater the number of florets in the bloom. A further consideration is that buds appearing early in long days tend to develop more vigorously over a longer period and therefore to contain more florets than buds of the same variety developing later in the season. Second crown blooms also frequently contain fewer florets for the reasons (a) that they usually develop later in the season than first crown, at a time when seasonal growth impetus in shorter days is beginning to decline, and (b) their laterals may be shorter and less vigorous. Furthermore, early buds initiated in long days tend to "hold" and develop the capitulum over a longer period, which means more florets, while late buds initiated in shorter days proceed to flowering more quickly over a shorter period, with fewer florets.

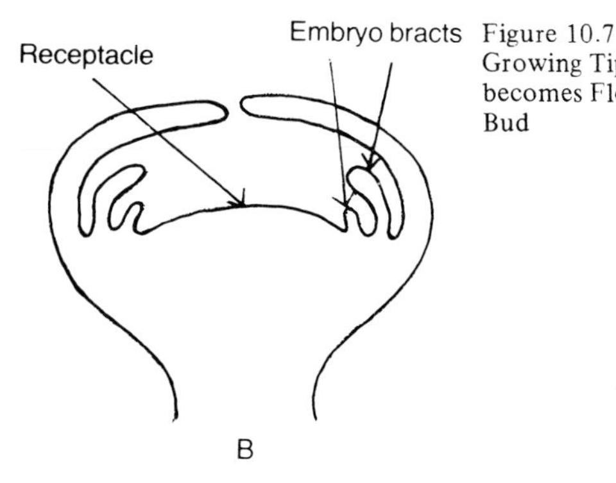

Figure 10.7 Growing Tip becomes Flower Bud

A = Growing tip of lateral

B = Same tip as flower bud is initiated—the shoot tip becomes the flower bud receptacle; embryo leaves become embryo bracts

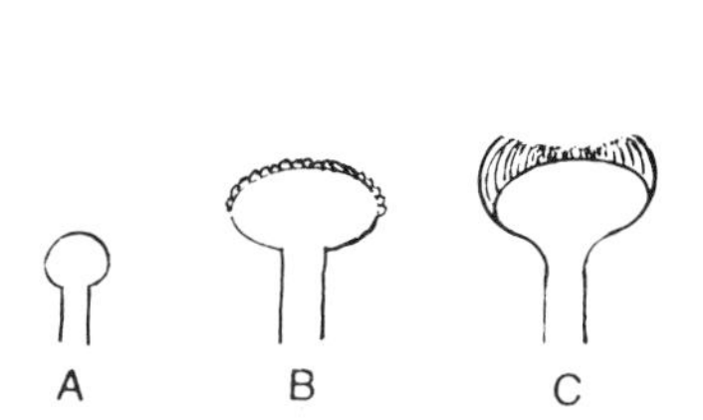

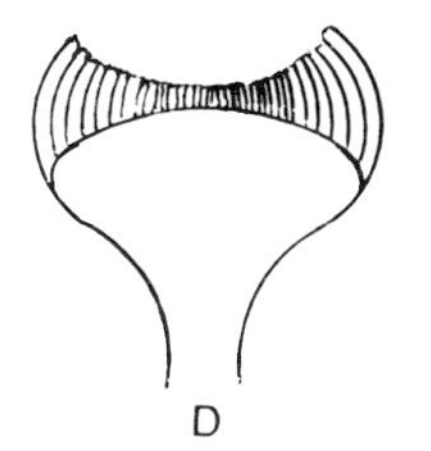

Figure 10.8 Bud Initiation to Colour Show

A = Embryo bud

B = Florets initiated

C = Florets in progressive development

D = Commencement of vacuolation in outer florets–central florets less advanced.

In the region of two weeks after bud initiation, which is some time before the bud is observed in the growing tip, embryo florets – no more than tiny "bumps" of tissue at this stage – will begin to develop on the receptacle, and a wave of floret inititiation will spread row by row over the following weeks from the base of the receptacle toward the crown until the entire receptacle is clothed with tiny embryo florets. By this time the bud is in most cases well visible and measures in the region of ⅛ in to ¼ in in diameter, with the lower florets more advanced in their development than those at the crown.

The plant is now entering an entirely different phase of development. While up to ten to fifteen leaves may develop after flower bud initiation, we must begin to turn our thoughts from vegetative to floret development and to do all we can to ensure that florets will develop to the full in terms of size and other aspects of bloom quality. By providing for the needs of healthy root activity, by ensuring a full leaf count and by calculated feeding the needs of long, strong laterals have been covered. Now it is time to look to the needs of the floret and the bloom.

Movement In The Bud

As has just been seen, florets are initiated row by row from the base of the receptacle to the crown over a period of several weeks, a shorter period in the case of small blooms with limited florets and a longer period in the case of large blooms with a considerable number of florets.

Following its initiation as a tiny cluster of cells a floret will grow initially by the process of "cell division", a cell dividing into two cells, with the process continuing for a period of, it is suggested, ten to fourteen days at a relatively rapid rate until the floret has developed its full quota of cells. Each row of florets on the receptacle will be subject to its phase of cell division as a wave of development spreads from the base of the receptacle to the crown.

Figure 10.9
Cell Division
and Vacuolation

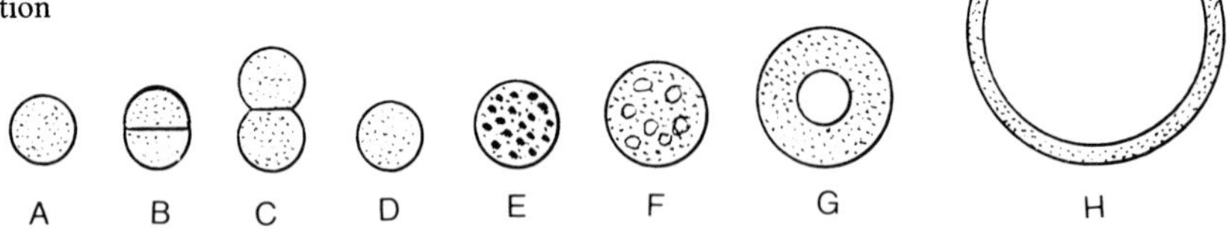

A = Newly formed cell

B = Same cell dividing

C = Newly formed cells

D = Newly formed cell expanding gradually

E = Cell expanding gradually with sugar-based deposits

F = Commencement of vacuolation, with a number of small vacuoles

G = Vacuoles merged, with protoplasm now lining cell wall

H = Completion of vacuolation

Although a large floret is said to contain several million cells, this early phase of floret development occurs in the bud, and when cell division is complete the floret is still tiny. Thus, floret cells at this stage are indeed ultra-microscopic. But it is in their numbers and composition that the size potential and quality of the floret, and therefore of the bloom, is basically determined.

Logically, a maximum number of cells is needed, for where all other factors are equal the greater the number of cells in a floret the greater its size potential; and if all the florets are large we shall enjoy large blooms.

Vigour of growth has a profound influence on cell division; the greater the vigour the higher the rate of cell division. Thus cell division is more likely to be rapid where a plant is growing strongly in long days of good light, and it is significant that experiments with other horticultural subjects have shown that feeds applied at the time of bud initiation have a greater effect on flower and fruit size than feeds applied at any other time; the reason is that feeds early in the bud accelerate the rate of growth just at the time when flower and fruit cells begin to divide. The principle holds good for chrysanthemums. Reasonable growth impetus is needed throughout the period of floret cell division – in other words during the period of bud development. But sugars exported from the leaves are also needed to considerable degree during cell division and for the further extension of the young cells, reinforcing the need to maintain the plant in balanced condition with leaves efficient exporters of their products.

Cell division commences in the first (lower) rows of florets when the bud is so tiny that it can hardly be seen, and it is therefore wrong to delay any planned "movement in the bud" until the bud is, say, ¼ in in diameter. Movement in the bud is desirable, but such movement must be no more than moderate and feeds should be reasonably balanced in terms of the three main nutrient elements, with "condition" still borne in mind. While bloom quality can be reduced by excessive nutrition *prior to the bud*, it can also be reduced by excessive nutrition *during the bud*. If a reasonably aerated fertile soil or compost has been prepared and the plants have developed strongly but in balance, the desired growth impetus in the bud can now be ensured without upsetting the "flowering condition" of the plant.

With pot plants three main factors can be employed. Where spare laterals are being carried their removal when tiny buds are in evidence, or just before, is calculated to gently boost vigour at the tips of the remaining laterals; a situation is suddenly created where a two-lateral root system is supplying only one lateral (in the case of large and medium exhibition plants), or (in the case of other disbuds), say, a three-lateral root system is supplying only two laterals. The removal of spare laterals does, in fact, result in a short period of extra vigour in the remaining laterals.

Then, we can switch to a slightly more active, more nitrogenous blend of fertiliser. Nothing drastic – just gentle persuasion! In the interests of full bloom size switch without pause to a preparation with approximately 50 per cent more nitrogen than phosphorus and potassium, using a powder with approximately 7.5 per cent nitrogen, 5 per cent phosphorus and 5 per cent potassium at a level teaspoon per week; or, where liquids are preferred, mix a preparation with 15 per cent nitrogen, 10 per cent phosphorus and 10 per cent potassium at a level tablespoon per gallon and apply it at a pint per week to each plant. It is interesting to note that in earlier days when reduction of nitrogen in the bud was being preached one of the most successful chrysanthemum fertilisers was already working along the lines we advocate.

Top Dressings

The third factor with pot plants is the extra growth impetus provided by compost top dressings. Final pots can be filled almost to the rim at the time of final potting and you can simply rely on feeding for the development of laterals and for the desired extra vigour in the bud; however, if extra space is allowed at the top of the pot at the time of final potting and periodic compost top dressings are applied, the continued extension of roots into new compost will be encouraged throughout the season, in a way similar to the continual extension of roots of earlies in an open soil. Extending roots produce growth-inducing hormones which are passed to growing tips to stimulate development, as well as taking up extra nutrients as they penetrate the new layers of compost. This obviously has an influence on vigour of growth, and growth is more likely to be balanced than if semi-dormant roots are more heavily fed.

Apply a ¼-in top dressing of John Innes No. 3 compost some six to seven weeks after final potting, repeating the dressing every two weeks, with a final ½-in dressing as soon as the tiny buds appear in the growing tips. Experiments indicate that such tactics lead to larger individual florets and therefore to larger blooms. The aim is to assist with the steady and continuous development of the long-V lateral, in condition, followed by movement in the bud.

Where soilless composts are in use, dressings should be applied at twice the depth to allow for subsequent settling of the more open medium.

Bud Movement To Earlies

Earlies can be similarly influenced by the removal of spare laterals and by a gentle nutrient boost, say a level teaspoon of powdered fertiliser (with the accent slightly on nitrogen), as soon as the tiny bud can be seen; as an alternative use a liquid feed. But the top dressing technique does not apply. Some growers resort to "mulching", however, covering the root area with well-rotted manure, spent mushroom compost, straw or peat in early July to conserve moisture and encourage surface rooting. We have rung the changes with these materials, and they certainly reduce the need of watering, but we have also seen "world beating" earlies produced without mulching.

Stems As A Barometer

Experienced growers apply a standard feeding programme, but modify it according to the known needs of particular varieties. They will have watched the vigour of the laterals; they will now be watching the colour, size and texture of the upper foliage. But they will also be watching the stems and, not least, stems developing beneath swelling buds. In fact, some of the best growers seem to study stems more than leaves, placing great store on their becoming "ripe", i.e. firm, the firmness gradually ascending the stem as the laterals develop. Experience tells them that where growth is too free, with stems bloated and soft beneath the bud, blooms can be disappointing. Movement under the bud as manifested by *slight* swelling of the stem may be desirable in that it indicates moderate vigour of growth, but excessive swell is generally undesirable.

Stems vary in girth and in colour according to the variety. Some have thin stems, some thick, but the characteristic is in no way related to inherent bloom size. Some have green stems, no matter what the cultural techniques and climatic conditions, while others darken or redden attractively, especially when temperatures are low. Some are at their best with a degree of stem swell and some are not. The discerning plantsman will look to his stems as barometers just as he does his leaves.

The need of "ripeness" has been recognised by many generations of chrysanthemum growers. In the British NCS Centenary Year Book A. Jarvis wrote: "It should be clearly understood that no good blooms can be obtained unless wood is ripened." But ripeness of growth is indicated by a firmness of stem rather than excessive hardness resulting from semi-starvation. The ideal lies between the extremes of soft, pliable or bloated stems and those which are hard and woody, and the ideal is achieved by controlled nutrition and watering only when the plant is in need.

How do you arrive at the ideal nutrient level for a particular variety? If a knowledgeable grower who has had experience of the variety will advise you this will save at least a season's experiment, but otherwise all you can do is grow the variety concerned on the standard diet and note the results. If it damps in the bloom (i.e. florets develop rotting patches) while other varieties on the same diet do not, it is obviously a variety which is soft in floret and the diet should be halved the following season. If you see better blooms at shows you should study their foliage and stems – if the leaves under the better blooms are larger and darker than yours, with stems thicker, the variety needs a more generous diet than the standard; if the leaves under the better blooms are smaller and paler, with stems thinner it obviously thrives on less. These are broad principles.

Where enough plants of a variety are grown you can learn a great deal about it by growing one-third of the batch on the standard diet, one-third on a half diet, and the other third on the standard diet but with 50 per cent increase in diet through the early bud period.

The End Of Routine Feeding

Routine feeding generally continues with pot plants up to the time of "calyx break", that is up to the time the bud-covering scales begin to break open. The residual effects of these feeds will continue to supply the needs of central florets still in the process of cell division.

Calyx break heralds the beginning of a further phase in the season's programme. The laterals have been built up, movement in the bud has been ensured, and now we come to the point of bloom development with its special considerations.

Temperature In The Bud Affects Bloom Quality

We have explained that excessive feeding can reduce bloom quality, and not least excessive feeding in the bud. Experiments have shown that temperature levels during the period of bud development can also have an appreciable affect on bloom quality. Night temperatures are especially important. Bloom size has been found to be markedly reduced at a night temperature of 60°F as opposed to 50°F *after the bud became visible*, and form and colour can be adversely affected by high temperatures. High night temperatures during bud development are indeed undesirable – 50°F is close to the ideal, and the fact should be borne in mind. Those growing in open surroundings with a free air circulation and well away from the close proximity of buildings are the more likely to enjoy the desired conditions.

Buds developing in long days of good light also produce larger blooms than those developing in shorter days. In other words, early buds produce larger blooms than those developing later in the season in shortening days.

Earwigs Can Damage Buds

During the period of bud swell keep watch for attacks by earwigs, which can so easily cause irreparable damage to the soft stems beneath buds and to the buds themselves. Insecticide powders tend to deter them and so, too, do waterings with a mild Jeyes solution between the plants. A further answer is to hand pick them from shoot tips and buds with a pair of tweezers by torchlight after dark. Yet another control is to apply a band of vaseline round stems beneath the buds as a barrier to their ascent. It is also necessary to continue to provide what is now routine control for mildew by fortnightly sprays with a mildew specific.

Another unwanted guest at this part of the season is the capsid bug. Capsids puncture stems beneath buds and growing tips to feed on the sap, and in so doing make vertical lesions which cause the shoot tip or bud to bend over. You can straighten stems by making several vertical slits with a penknife in the soft tissues opposite the wound. Capsids also cause shoot tips to become blind and they damage buds so that blooms are disfigured. The smaller blunt-headed froghopper, which springs from the plant as one approaches, is said to cause similar damage, but we have never been able to substantiate the claim and regard the capsid bug as a far more serious pest.

CHAPTER 11

Flowering the Earlies

Plenty of early-flowering chrysanthemums will stand up to the wind and rain of the British autumn without protection, so long as they are properly staked, and many growers do not resort to protection. Incurves and intermediates hold rain in their upturned florets, but most of them tolerate the inconvenience with little more than interference with bloom form, while reflexes are designed to shed the rain, and in fact a good downpour can even improve their form. Outdoor sprays are seldom protected.

Figure 11.1 Blooms in Polythene Bags

It has to be said, however, that the very best blooms of earlies are more likely to be enjoyed where some form of cover is provided, and for this reason the more dedicated growers and exhibitors provide protection during the flowering period, either in the form of large overhead covers or by resort to the bagging of individual blooms with bloom bags.

In most cases overhead covers of glass, glass-substitute, PVC or polythene are sufficient, but in some urban districts the best way to obtain clean whites and yellows is to bag them. Yellows hold their colour well in bags, but pinks, reds, bronzes and purples are reduced in colour and are not really suited to bagging – even clear polythene bags will cause colour reduction. The high temperatures created in closed bags is the main cause of colour loss. The pigments responsible for yellow colouration are more stable, and heat has little effect on them. We have recorded temperatures 50°F higher in bags than the ordinary shade temperature at the time.

Ideally, temperatures would be in the region of 60° to 65°F by day and 50°F at night, and the less they rise above these levels the better the bloom colour. Form and size can also be adversely affected by heat during flowering. Incurves and intermediates may develop in their true form at slightly higher temperatures, but reflexes tend to be more sleek in form at lower rather than higher levels. Some varieties fail to develop their central florets fully under high night temperatures and produce blooms with small, quilled central florets; some growers of exhibition earlies go so far as to operate cold fans beneath their large overhead covers to keep cool air moving between their plants. Another point which the exhibitor will need to bear in mind is that "coloured" varieties often lose colour on the side nearest the sun and some form of shading is therefore advantageous.

Covering has three aims: protection from the adverse effects of wind, rain and sun.

Overhead Covers

Overhead covers should be substantial enough and sufficiently well secured to stand up to gales, and posts should be driven at least a foot into the ground. They can be large sloping structures designed to shed the rain and cover the whole plot or they can be designed to cover smaller blocks of plants.

Growers frequently improvise from materials on hand, but polythene or corrugated PVC sheeting are the most popular covering mediums. Polythene should be of stout gauge and secured to spars at frequent intervals. In the interests of moderate temperatures it is also advisable to underlay the polythene with butter muslin or something similar. Heavy shading should be avoided, however, for the colour pigment in pinks, reds, bronzes and purples which is adversely affected by heat also needs light for its development, and heavy shading can reduce colour just as effectively as high temperature. So the aim has to be reasonable light and moderate temperatures.

The time to erect covers is when the scales covering the buds begin to break. At this stage make a final check for secure staking,

Figure 11.2
A Simple Overhead
Cover for Protecting
Earlies

Figure 11.3
Bud Ready for
Protection

then make a thorough inspection for pests. Pay particular attention to the buds themselves, for aphids are sometimes hidden beneath their curled-up bracts and it pays to inspect them carefully and to apply a dusting of insecticide powder. Nicotine powder is especially effective.

Erect the covers well clear of buds, with a decided tilt toward the prevailing wind where flat covers are in use, and allow sufficient overhang to protect outer blooms.

Bags

Well-grown vases of whites and yellows which have been bagged take some beating on the showbench. Several types of bag are available, mostly made of waterproof paper, or of polythene pierced with tiny holes; specially manufactured wire frames are often used to support them and prevent them chafing the blooms.

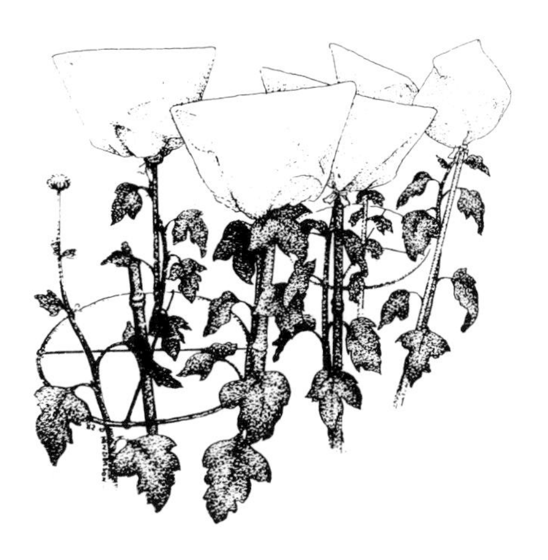

Figure 11.4
Bags over Buds of Earlies

The time to bag is at the first sign of bloom colour. Before bagging, inspect buds for pests and dust them with nicotine or some other insecticide powder. Where wire frames are to be used, fit the frame first, then pull the bag over the frame and shape round the stem at the neck, securing with a wire twist or garden twine. Where frames are not used blow up the bag, shape at the neck before fitting, then place over the bud and mould round the stem before tying. Buds of incurves and intermediates should be a little below centre in the bag and buds of reflexes a little above centre. Thin stems should be provided with a thin cane right up to the bud. Write the date of covering on a corner of each bag – in pencil – as a guide to when blooms should be fully developed.

Bagging may be looked upon as a tedious operation, but when almost perfect unblemished blooms are revealed and staged in a vase it is all well worth while.

Double-bag For "Pinking"

Whites and yellows sometimes "pink" badly at the base, even when protected by bags. But the defect can be cured by resort to "double bagging". The method is as follows: insert one bloom bag inside the other, then 4 in or so from the open end of the outer bag pierce a few "drainage holes" with a pencil. Blow up the bags, then dip the necks in a bucket of water, shake off the surplus, open up the neck and position over the bud, gathering the moist ends together and moulding them closely round the stem. Tie tightly with wire twists or garden twine, with a second tie well up the neck of the bag. If properly carried out the bags will remain inflated in all weathers. Any rain penetrating the outer bag will escape through the drainage holes.

Pinking is caused by the cold, and double bags act as insulators against extreme temperature falls on cold nights. If you can maintain a reasonable temperature level you will have whites and yellows free of pinking.

Watering, Pests And The Notebook

Roots should now be kept more evenly moist – not waterlogged, but certainly not parched. Apply a moderate watering several times a week if the weather is dry and where covers keep rain away from the roots.

Make frequent inspections for the presence of pests, especially aphids, earwigs and caterpillars in developing blooms. The first sign of earwigs and caterpillars is often their small droppings on florets or, in the case of large caterpillars, the odd floret which has been nibbled through and fallen to the floor. The bud-split dusting with insecticide powder will have done much to control aphids, but as a last resort you can go so far as to thoroughly spray infested blooms with mild insecticide solution, preferably with a steady breeze blowing on a sunless day.

Bloom Feeding

In years gone by it was unthinkable that one would feed earlies – indeed any chrysanthemum – when they were in flower, but experiments have shown that what is now referred to as "bloom feeding" can be advantageous in many cases.

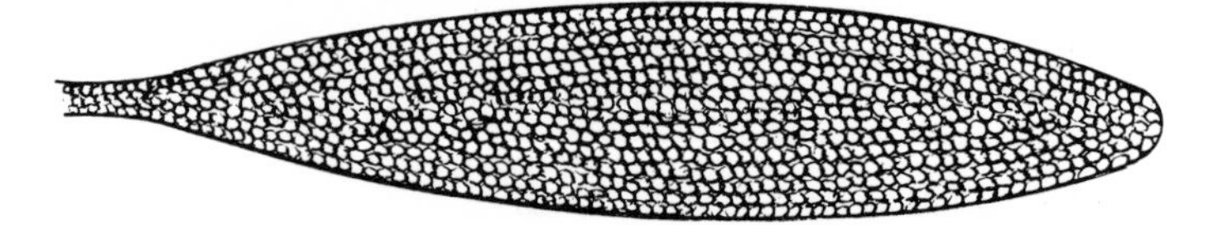

Figure 11.5
A Floret is Composed of Millions of Cells

All that is happening when a bloom unfolds is that the tiny cells which were packed into the florets in the bud swell period are now expanding – in much the same way as a balloon becomes larger when it is blown up. In the case of floret cells they are expanding and filling with plant sap, and extra nutrition at the time of expansion can lead to cells – and therefore florets and blooms – becoming larger.

Bloom feeding can take two forms. It can consist of either (a) mild feeding from the time of colour show to bloom maturity, or (b) later and rather more intensive feeding from the point of, say, one-third development of the bloom through to maturity.

Fertilisers used for bloom feeding must be quick acting and this means that they should be applied in solution. A preparation containing 20 per cent nitrogen, 10 per cent phosphorus and 10 per cent potassium is regarded as close to the ideal. Where bloom feeding to earlies commences at colour show it should be used at a level teaspoon per gallon twice a week, giving each plant a quart at each feed. Feeding should continue until bloom maturity. Where feeding commences later, but is more intensive, the solution should be prepared at a level dessertspoon to the gallon, commencing feeding when blooms are approximately one-third developed and continuing to bloom maturity, again at a quart per plant twice per week.

Three considerations are of interest. First, bloom feeding will not fully compensate for earlier deficiencies and turn a poor bloom into a good bloom – it will merely help – and where plants have been grossly overfed they will have little beneficial effect, for the plant is in no condition to profit from them. This is why plants need to be in "flowering condition". Expanding cells can only enlarge to the full where sugars are in ample supply. Where plants have been overfed and leaves are dark and gross, floret cells will be supplied with too little sugar, and no amount of bloom feeding will compensate (see p. 93). So, plants need to be in good condition for full response to bloom feeding.

Second, one should be wary of any drastic stimulation to, say, the upper florets of incurves and tight intermediates. Any bloom feeding to these should be uniform throughout bloom opening, to avoid tiered development. On the other hand, late boosts to reflexes can broaden small florets emerging from the central button and produce impressive and sleek shoulders.

Third, it is our experience that bloom feeding does not cause damping. Where damping occurs it is invariably due to too much feed in the pre-bud and bud phases or to excessive atmospheric humidity during bloom development. We have succeeded in convincing many doubters of this over recent years. Where bloom feeding commences at colour show the mild solution recommended should in no way lead to damping, and where the stronger solution is used damping is unlikely if feeding is delayed until blooms are one-third developed and many florets in active development are sharing the feed. In fact, growers have used much stronger solutions than we are advising and taken their blooms to the National shows at London and secured coveted first prize cards.

More Stock Selection

We now begin to savour the thrill of good blooms – and the disappointment of failures. In both cases make a note of any special treatment which may have contributed to such results, especially where nutrition is concerned. If notes are kept, keep the columns of the notebook up to date with a weekly round for dates of colour show, full bloom, etc.

Plants producing blooms of exceptional merit should be so labelled. These will provide the stools from which next year's plants should be taken. Those producing poor results or suspect from the point of view of aspermy virus or other serious diseases should be taken up and burned. On no account should they be used for stock.

Continue with the removal of belated sideshoots and with the trimming of basal shoots to soil level.

Exhibition Dates – "Secret" Preparation

Exhibitors will have made diary notes of show dates and final dates for entries, and will be watching the development of possible exhibits. A week or so before blooms are to be cut for the show spray the upper surface of the leaves with an oil-based insecticide solution, taking care to keep it off the blooms. Foliage so treated will stand out against that of its untreated neighbours in the exhibition hall. We have, in fact, been asked by visitors to shows whether we polished the leaves of our exhibits.

Cleanliness And Tidiness

As blooms come and go remove old leaves, especially those infested with pests and mildew. Also clean and store canes and covers; do not leave them on the plot to deteriorate. In short, keep the plot generally tidy and free of pest-harbouring debris.

Retain a central cane to each stool up to the time of lifting, to prevent plants rocking in high wind or at worst breaking off at the crown. This is a real danger where heavy top growth develops after flowering – and keep such top growth free of pests and diseases, continuing with at least a fortnightly insecticide spray if pests are prevalent. Keep watch, too, for slugs. They can inflict serious damage at this time of year and by so doing make serious inroads into next year's supply of cuttings.

CHAPTER 12

Flowering Lates

House Between Bud-break And Colour Show

Lates are normally taken into the greenhouse for flowering soon after the scales covering the buds have begun to break, and before they have developed a complete fringe of bloom colour. This is usually in the second half of September, with large exhibition plants being taken in first, followed by incurves, reflexes and intermediates, and finally singles.

Plants housed before they have reached calyx break, with their stems still soft and lengthening beneath the buds, tend to run up after housing and to develop long necks with inferior blooms. In fact some growers bag the buds and delay housing until later in the month to make sure that stems thoroughly ripen up to the bud.

Advance Preparation

The greenhouse must be thoroughly cleaned down a week or so beforehand. Remove everything, then wash the framework and glass with a Jeyes solution mixed at two tablespoons per gallon, or with a similar disinfectant. A few days later fumigate the house for both pests and diseases, using a smoke cone or pellets, or a sulphur candle.

Some form of shading will be necessary during the flowering period to keep temperatures down in sunshine. This can consist of a shading spray to the glass or a lining of butter muslin fitted beneath the glass. Wherever it is practicable, the latter is preferable as it further constitutes an insulating secondary layer against temperature extremes, and this can prevent the pinking of whites and yellows close to the glass in cold spells.

The Housing Procedure

Housing should be carried out systematically. Water the plants well the day before, remove any withering lower leaves, particularly those below the point of the stop, trim basal growths as necessary, and then finally stake with canes and ties well up to the buds. Spray thoroughly with a combined insecticide/fungicide solution, and when almost dry remove the plants carefully from their straining wires and carry them into the greenhouse pot first to avoid damaging them. Any spare laterals should have been removed earlier, of course, but where weaklings remain which are obviously incapable of producing quality blooms they too should be removed.

Pots should stand on a base which ensures good drainage. The ideal is a layer of shingle some two inches deep over the whole greenhouse floor, which not only provides for good drainage but also facilitates the levelling of pots and even spacing of buds. Ideally, spacing would be such that the leaves of neighbouring plants do not touch, but this is usually impracticable, and in order to make full use of the available space the best you can do is to ensure that blooms will have ample room for their development. We have ourselves of necessity packed in plants much closer than we would have preferred with little apparent inconvenience as far as results are concerned.

Plants should be arranged with an eye to the best effect during the flowering period, with the tallest at the end opposite the door and with height gradually falling to the door end. It is often suggested that developing blooms should be no closer than 12 in or so to the glass or butter muslin lining. In amateur houses this is again all too often impracticable, and where greenhouse management is properly controlled, with a satisfactory air circulation and temperature levels, blooms will develop close to a muslin lining with no harmful effect.

The First Ten To Fourteen Days

For the first ten to fourteen days full ventilation should be provided night and day, except in gales, frost and fog. The aim should be to accustom the plants gradually to their new surroundings, and routine supplementary heating is not yet needed. Where possible the air should be kept moving gently between the plants by means of a fan or fans. But in the event of hard frost provide just sufficient warmth to prevent damage to opening buds.

Keep Them Evenly Moist

Housed plants should be kept more evenly moist at the roots – but not too moist. The watering routine is much the same as previously, except that water is given more frequently and in smaller quantities, say, a cupful or half a pint as soon as the surface of the compost begins to dry. Both overwatering and wilting followed by heavier applications must be avoided. Preferably water during the morning, and not later than midday. Water straight from the tap will be suitable, but if water is ice cold in cans which have been standing out add a little hot water and stir it in with a cane.

After housing, you should water direct from the spout of the can, with the rose removed, in order to avoid unnecessary splashing. Later, as the flowers begin to open it is desirable to keep humidity within bounds; it is then in particular that early watering and the avoidance of splashing is desirable.

Late Feeding — With Liquids Only

Powder feeds to pot plants normally cease at colour show, and in earlier days this was when all feeding came to an end. But times and outlooks have changed and, as with the earlies, many growers of lates now resort to bloom feeding. The considerations and tactics are exactly the same as for earlies (see p. 108), with either (a) a mild feed from the time of colour show to bloom maturity, or (b) later and more intensive feeding from the point of one-third development of the bloom through to maturity. Again a preparation containing 20 per cent nitrogen, 10 per cent phosphorus and 10 per cent potassium is recommended, with method (a) at a level teaspoon per gallon and method (b) at a dessertspoon per gallon, but in this case liquid feeds are given in the place of clear water; in other words bloom feeding to pot plants is a continuous process as opposed to two applications per week in the case of earlies in the open ground.

As with the earlies, much stronger feeding has been used to advantage on occasion, even to the extent of a level teaspoon of the neat powder to a pot ten days before a show. But this should be regarded as experimental and more likely to be successful with reflexes. It should not be indulged in haphazardly.

Pests And Diseases — Fumigate In Outbreaks

Keep watch for pests, especially for earwigs and aphids in opening blooms. Earwigs can be handpicked from blooms with tweezers by torchlight after dark; where serious aphid infestation is threatened fumigation will be necessary. At the correct concentration modern fumigants can be used without damage to blooms, but the manufacturer's instructions must be followed to the letter.

Mildew is the disease most likely to be troublesome under glass, but where spraying has been thoroughly carried out with a fungicide prior to housing no problem should arise. If mildew does build up, however, use can be made of a fungicidal fumigant.

Frequent Inspection

Check plants thoroughly at least weekly for developing sideshoots, withering lower leaves and damaged florets. Remove them as they occur. If florets begin to shatter examine the affected bloom carefully. The trouble may be due to a caterpillar; it may be due to bud rot, caused by the fungus Ray Blight; or damage may be due to overfeeding prior to the bud or in the bud swell period.

Periodic trimming of basal growths should continue, with the final trim ten to twelve weeks before the planned rooting date for next season.

For those intent on exhibiting it may be helpful to gently manipulate florets here and there as blooms develop, and certainly distorted or damping florets should be removed either by hand or with a pair of tweezers. Late-flowering singles sometimes develop ray florets in the central disc. These should be carefully withdrawn early in their development to enable the disc florets to close over the gap. Some growers of singles turn their pots every few days to ensure even development and blooms which are upright on their stems. This is also a sound tactic with multi-flowered late-flowering sprays with blooms well down the stem, and the same could be said for charms and large specimen plants. Their cultivation will be covered in more detail in Chapter 15.

Ventilation Reduced; Temperature Raised

As outside temperatures fall and blooms begin to open, ventilation should be gradually reduced and artificial heat becomes increasingly necessary. A temperature of 60° to 65°F is ample by day, though the level is bound to rise in sunshine, and 50°F is sufficient at night. Ventilate freely by day beyond these levels in all but strong winds and fog, even to the extent of having the door wide open.

Extremes should still be avoided. Under excessively high temperatures blooms lack colour and lustre, and some varieties may fail to develop satisfactorily in the centre. At low temperatures incurves may become loose at the base and the open type of intermediate may tend to reflex, but low temperatures can promote sleek form in reflexes.

The Danger Of Damping

So much for ideal temperatures. But there is a further important consideration, namely bloom damping, with temperature control the one effective weapon against it.

Some varieties are inherently prone to damping and excess feeding in the growth and bud phases makes damping more likely. Another factor, however, and one which must be watched carefully during bloom development, is atmospheric humidity.

Hygrometers, instruments which indicate the level of atmospheric humidity, are used by many growers of late-flowering chrysanthemums to assist with humidity control. These instruments show that in sunny weather the atmosphere is relatively dry, at 50 per cent humidity or below, and when this is so ventilators and doors can be opened wide, even when blooms are well developed, without any risk of damping. But on dull, wet days humidity can be up to 90 per cent, which is well above the danger mark – a reasonably safe level is 70 per cent.

Fortunately, warmth can be used to reduce atmospheric moisture; an increase in temperature of 5°F reduces humidity by approximately 10 per cent. If we therefore assume that the normal night humidity reading would reach 90 per cent it means that a 10°F rise in temperature above the outside level (at night and on dull, damp days) is needed to keep humidity at no more than 70 per cent. In fact, this is a sound outlook. If at night and on dull, humid days a temperature level 10°F above that of the outside air is maintained, you will suffer virtually no trouble from damping.

While the ideal night temperature in respect of overall bloom quality may be 50°F, and while 50°F may be better for the form of reflexes and nearer 60°F for incurves, such levels can only be provided when outside conditions permit. The temperature must always be 10°F higher at night and on humid days, whatever this means in terms of the greenhouse temperature. If the night temperature outside is 55°F the temperature inside must be 65°F, and the same applies by day in muggy spells. Happy the grower in a district with cool night temperatures who can put on the necessary heat and yet remain close to temperature ideals.

One of the main causes of damping is the germination of Botrytis and other floret-invading fungus spores, and we are told by specialists in this field that they will germinate and penetrate plant tissues to initiate damping if the atmosphere is sufficiently humid for their germination for a period of eight hours; under ideal conditions the period can be as short as three hours. In other words, one night of excessive humidity can lead to widespread damping. The lesson is clear!

Obviously everything possible must be done to prevent excessive moisture in the greenhouse and watering should be carried out early in the day to allow for the evaporation and escape before nightfall of surface moisture. Care should also be taken to avoid splashing between the pots; it is for this reason that the rose is removed and water is applied direct from the spout of the can in the flowering season.

Heating Methods

There are, of course, many ways of heating greenhouses, but perhaps that most widely employed by the amateur chrysanthemum grower today is the electric fan heater. This propels heat gently round the house and is invariably controlled by a sensitive thermostat which will click on and off through the night within a degree or two of its setting.

We have experimented at length with the management of amateur greenhouses during the flowering period and would suggest you consider the following routine. During flowering close down the roof vents at night except for an inch or two on, say, the two roof vents furthest from the door. Leave two inches of air on the door and position the fan heater a foot above floor level 2 or 3 ft inside the door with a large steadily revolving cold fan positioned a foot or so in front of it. This will ensure that air entering the house is warmed by the heater and then circulates between the plants before filtering to atmosphere through the roof vents at the far end of the house. The roof vents should be covered with butter muslin, and so too should the upper half of the door entrance. The small amount of ventilation maintained ensures a steady circulation of warm air between blooms and prevents the build-up of internal humidity. In practice the method words extremely well, and yet economically. On damp days maintain these settings, but when the air is dry increase ventilation by day up to full air on all vents and the door in sunshine. In other words, provide as much ventilation as possible so long as the air is not too humid.

Where there is no supply of electricity much can be done even with paraffin heaters. While they need regular attention, they at least automatically keep the inside temperature so many degrees above that outside, which tends to prevent damping.

So much detail may give the impression that the management of greenhouse chrysanthemums during the flowering period is somewhat tedious and complicated. In fact, with thought and a little experience the activity becomes a pleasant daily routine. The points to bear in mind can be condensed quite simply: (a) water lightly early in the day; (b) keep temperatures as close to the stated ideals as possible, but always 10°F or so above the outside level; (c) keep watch for pests and bloom defects.

Stock Selection

As blooms mature label those plants which produce something special as stock plants for the coming season. There will be other things to note, more especially if you visit shows and other growers and see blooms which are obviously better than your own. Ask questions of other growers with a view to better things next year. If damping occurs it could well be that you may have overfed a particular variety. Coarseness can similarly be due to excessive nutrition or early buds, while lack of size can be due to poor root action or late buds. "Daisy eye" can also be caused by late buds, and where this occurs you should plan for earlier rooting and earlier stopping next season.

CHAPTER 13

Exhibition

Not everyone is by nature an exhibitor, but exhibitions are in some ways the backbone of the chrysanthemum movement. Nothing has done more to foster interest and stimulate the development of better and better varieties and improved methods of cultivation. It is on the show table that you will come to grips with the finer points of quality and discover how good your blooms really are and just how sound your methods. A mental picture of the blooms at home so often surpasses the prizewinners on the show bench, but how different it might have been if they were placed side by side!

The exhibitor is exhibiting with other enthusiasts as well as competing against them. In a season or two rivals become firm friends with a genuine regard for each other's wellbeing. So consider joining your local specialist society, and why not the National Chrysanthemum Society? Put in the odd vase and enjoy yourself. One should at least think of paying a visit to the shows and chatting to other growers. If you do exhibit, your first vases may not be among the top prizes, but they should get better and better until they eventually stand with the best.

National Chrysanthemum Society Rules And Registrations

The chrysanthemum classes in all but small mixed shows are judged under National Chrysanthemum Society rules by judges who have passed an examination and are registered with that body. The adjudicators are chrysanthemum experts and judging is therefore to a high standard.

Each variety is assessed in accordance with its classification in the NCS Register. In this publication those varieties registered by the NCS Floral Committee are listed according to type, form, size, colour, etc., and they must be so exhibited. Thus, large blooms are exhibited against large, reflexed against reflexed, singles against singles, and so on. Only registered varieties are eligible for competitive classes judged under NCS rules. The various sections of the classification system are listed in Chapter 1. Bear in mind that only varieties from Sections 13-30 are eligible for early-flowering shows and Sections 1-20 for late-flowering shows. If you are in doubt on any point of classification and exhibiting, the Secretary of any society with chrysanthemum classes in its schedule should be able to help you or put you in touch with someone who can.

Good Blooms – Technical Points

What constitutes a quality bloom, and what are the judges looking for?

The important qualities are full size, neat form, crisp freshness and good colour. In addition, foliage is taken into account, so too is staging; uniformity of size, colour and form between the blooms of a particular variety is also considered.

For those intent on more serious exhibition the National Chrysanthemum Society's book "Chrysanthemum Judging and Exhibiting" is a must. In brief: *size* is assessed relative to what is regarded as normal full size for the variety; *form* requirements are relative to the form classification of the variety; blooms should be completely *fresh*, with no signs of basal "tiredness"; *colour* should be what is described as "good colour for the variety"; blooms of any one variety in an exhibit should be *uniform* in size, form (including stage of development) and colour; *foliage* should be clean, undamaged and free of pests and diseases; *staging*, i.e. the presentation of blooms in their vases, should be such that each bloom stands on its own and yet in balanced arrangement, preferably with foliage covering the top of the vase.

At the time of writing a two-year trial period is commencing to allow the staking of disbudded blooms with unobtrusive supports.

Large exhibition – Full size and freshness is regarded as especially important in this section. To have both is a challenge. In matters of form, a variety is judged as presented – if a bloom has reflexed it will be so judged, if it has been produced in intermediate form it will be judged as an intermediate. In the interests of maintaining bloom freshness, foliage may be removed and a substitute stem of foliage fitted. Stem supports may be used, and to facilitate the presentation of blooms to best effect, wire ring supports may be employed unobtrusively beneath blooms to spread the florets to produce a pleasing balance between breadth and depth.

Medium exhibition – Similar to large exhibition, but smaller. Requirements and assessments are as for large exhibition. Foliage may again be removed, and stem supports and wire rings to support the florets are permitted.

Incurved – Incurved blooms should be spherical in form. They should be nicely closed at the centre, firm and fresh, with florets closely laid. A large bloom of loose petallage is inferior to a smaller bloom of close, even petallage. Lower "skirting" florets which give a ragged appearance at the base should be removed. Incurves with a depressed crown are inferior to those finished with a full centre which contributes to the spherical outline when viewed from the side. Flat-topped and conically-shaped blooms are inferior to those of true spherical form.

Reflexed – Again, blooms should have breadth and depth in equal proportion. They should certainly not be shallow and platelike. With varieties of classical reflexed form the florets should fall gracefully from the crown to overlap one another evenly, without gaps, to produce a smooth contour. Some reflexes have a central "button" of undeveloped florets – this should be circular. Others lack the central button and develop their florets from a more bristly central zone. In both cases blooms should be exhibited at what is loosely referred to as the "seven-eighths" stage of development, with an area of young florets still to unfurl.

Intermediate – Broadly speaking, this section covers types not eligible for the incurved and reflexed sections, and bloom formation is somewhat variable. Some varieties are incurving, building up to a loose ball, either with a closed top or with a depressed crown; some are reflexing in the lower florets and incurving in the upper florets; some are of more quilled or spiky petallage. In each case breadth and depth should be near to equal.

Anemones – The central disc is of particular importance with this type. The disc (or central "cushion") should be fresh, deep and evenly constituted and fully developed. Florets may be flat or quilled.

Singles – Florets of singles should emerge at right-angles to the stem, though they may reflex or incurve at the tips. Central discs should be circular, clean and uniform in their stage of development.

Pompons – Blooms should be ball-shaped in the case of "true poms" and half-round with a flat base in the case of "semi-poms". Blooms should be even in size, even in development, fresh, nicely spaced and uniform in colour.

Sprays – For purposes of exhibition two types of sprays are recognised (a) the "terminal" spray with one bloom on a "pedicel" (short flower stem), and (b) the "compound" spray, which can have more than one bloom on a pedicel. Blooms should be even in size, development and colour, they should be evenly spaced without congestion at the crown and with, for preference, blooms emerging well down the stem, especially in the case of late-flowering sprays.

Specimen plants in pots – Specimen plants should have a large number of evenly developed quality blooms, with clean, healthy foliage. Blooms should be nicely spaced, with the training framework and ties as unobtrusive as possible. The plant should be balanced with blooms facing all round.

Vases, bowls and baskets arranged for effect – Exhibits should be lightly and pleasingly arranged so that every bloom can be observed separately. Overcrowding is a serious fault. Blooms should be of good quality and fresh in texture.

Judging Is Based On A Points System

Points systems are laid down by the National Chrysanthemum Society as the basis of all judging. Those applying to disbud exhibits and sprays are as follows:

Table A
THe following pointings are applicable to Sections 3, 4, 5, 6, 7, 10, 11, 13, 14, 15, 16, 17, 20, 23, 24, 25, 26, 27, and 30 – and to Sections 8, 9, 18, 19, 28 and 29 when shown as individual blooms:

Form	25
Size	20
Freshness	20
Colour	15
Uniformity between blooms of a variety	10
Foliage	5
Staging	5
	100

Table B
The following pointings are applicable to Sections 1 and 2:

Form	25
Size	30
Freshness	30
Colour	10
Staging and foliage	5
	100

Table C
The following pointings are applicable to classes for exhibition "terminal" sprays for Sections 8, 9, 18, 19, 28 and 29:

Spray Form:	
Uniform placement and development of blooms	20
Breadth and depth (balance)	15
Number of blooms	10
Bloom Quality:	
Form	15
Freshness	15
Colour	10
Size	5
Foliage and stems	5
Staging	5
	100

Table D
The following points are applicable to classes calling for "stems of sprays" and eligible to both "terminal" and "compound" sprays from Sections 8, 9, 18, 19, 28 and 29:

Bloom quality (form, size, freshness, colour)	35
Depth and breadth of sprays	30
Staging, overall effect and balance of vase	30
Foliage and stems	5
	100

Other types such as charms, specimens, bowls and baskets, etc., are covered by special tables, which can be found in the National Chrysanthemum Society's book on exhibiting.

Other national societies have somewhat different rules and requirements, but in all cases the principles are similar.

Study Schedules In Advance

Study show schedules well in advance and make a note of any special local rules and the final date for acceptance of entries. When the time comes for filling in the entry form make sure that you have the correct classification for each of your varieties. What appears to be a bronze, due to the predominance of the colour of the underside (or reverse) of the florets may be classified as a red, and what you look upon as a purple may be a deep pink.

Form is variable in some varieties, and an intermediate which has developed either as a reflex or incurve can be shown in classes for intermediates or reflexes or incurves, but an incurve which reflexes cannot be shown as a reflex, nor can a reflex which incurves be shown as an incurve or intermediate.

Practise At Home

Few self-respecting exhibitors stage their blooms without a measure of titivating – and rightly so. While the manipulation and presenting of blooms out of character for the variety may not be acceptable, a certain amount of tidying is to be recommended. Untidy centres of reflexes are greatly improved if the young and still incurving florets close to the central button are turned carefully over into the reflexing form. This can be carried out with broad, smooth-ended tweezers or even with the butt of a knitting needle and the fingers. Others work with cotton buds from the chemist. Damaged florets should be removed, and others coaxed into place to fill gaps in the floret lay. Untidy "skirting" florets should be removed from the base of incurves and incurving intermediates. Foliage should be cleaned.

It is also a sound tactic to practise staging at home. Try staging one in a vase, then three in a vase with two blooms at the back and one in front, then on to five in a vase with three blooms at the back and two at the front. Stage at an overall height of about 24 in for the central bloom at the back of a vase of five, with the flanking blooms a little lower; front blooms should be 3 or 4 in lower still. Space blooms an inch or so apart, so that they are seen separately and yet appear as a composite group, not overcrowded, but not widely separated. Newspaper can be pressed between stems to bring them into the desired position, but any packing should be hidden from view by the foliage spilling nicely over the top of the vase. And make sure your blooms are facing to the front. So often when judging one comes across blooms turned the wrong way for no apparent reason and to the detriment of the exhibit.

Figure 13.1
An Unprepared Reflex

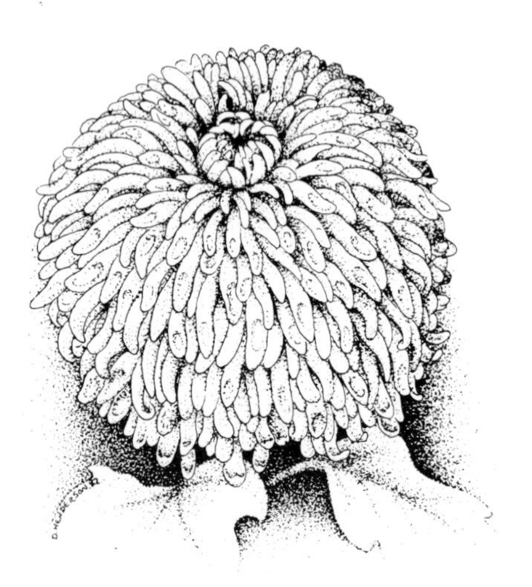

Figure 13.2
The Same Bloom Tidied at the Crown for Exhibition

Where blooms are not ideally matched, those with extra depth should be positioned in the back row, where the extra depth will be seen to advantage. Stage more shallow blooms at the front where there is a tendency to view them from above. This will not fool the judge, but it helps the general effect.

Showtime

If you have to cancel an entry let the show officials know as soon as possible, but honour your entry if you can make up a worthwhile exhibit. It is often said that it is the losers who make a show. Certainly we cannot all be winners, and with no losers there would be no show.

Begin cutting and preliminary dressing in plenty of time; do not leave it for a last minute scramble. It is unfair to your flowers, to yourself and to the show to cut at the last minute, then to bunch blooms together, rush to the exhibition hall and just plop them in a vase.

Damp spots sometimes develop in florets after removal to the storage buckets, and for this reason alone it is advisable to cut in plenty of time. Defective florets can then be removed well before staging, or other blooms can be substituted.

If the ground is at all dry, water earlies the day before cutting. Blooms should be cut while fresh and crisp and on no account while in a wilting condition. The best time is early morning, when the plants are well charged with moisture, but this is not always convenient, and many growers have to cut in the evening. In this event wait until the sun is off the plants and blooms are turgid, and preferably some 36 hours before the show.

Before commencing cutting, stand deep buckets or drums of water, in a cool, light, airy room or shed where the sun cannot fall on the blooms. Deep florist's buckets with almost vertical sides are suitable, but old drums, thoroughly cleaned, make good substitutes. Domestic buckets with sloping sides allow the blooms to lean outward and to possibly topple, but a half-brick on wire netting in the bottom will prevent this happening.

Cut blooms vase by vase, allowing a spare to each. Incurves should be fully developed; some reflexed and intermediate varieties should have more to come in the centre. Blooms of "double" varieties showing a "blown" centre or a central disc (referred to as "daisy eye") are not worthy of consideration. Whites and yellows should be clean, without any sign of "pinking" on the lower florets. Each vase should be planned to consist of blooms uniform in size, colour and development. An odd monster unbalances the vase and detracts from its smaller partners. It is better to have five matched smaller blooms, than four small and one large.

Use secateurs for cutting, then crush the bottom 4 in of stem with a hammer or pair of pliers to assist water uptake. Cut to about 24 inches, and as each bloom is cut examine it superficially for damaged florets. Remove the foliage from large exhibition varieties at the time of cutting – duplicate stems of foliage will be needed and these too should be cut and placed in water to be fitted at the time of staging.

Do not hurry cutting. If you have too much to cope with enlist the aid of a careful assistant.

Advance Dressing

It helps considerably if advanced dressing can be carried out at home, where it can be done in comfort, without interruption or distraction. Dress vase by vase plus the spare. The amount of dressing needed varies greatly with the variety. Some hardly need touching, but with others it can be a tedious process. Work from the base upward with reflexed blooms, and from the top downward with incurving and incurves, removing damaged florets and those which interfere with symmetry, moving others gently into position to present an even contour to the bloom without offensive gaps. Any defective florets should be drawn out cleanly with tweezers.

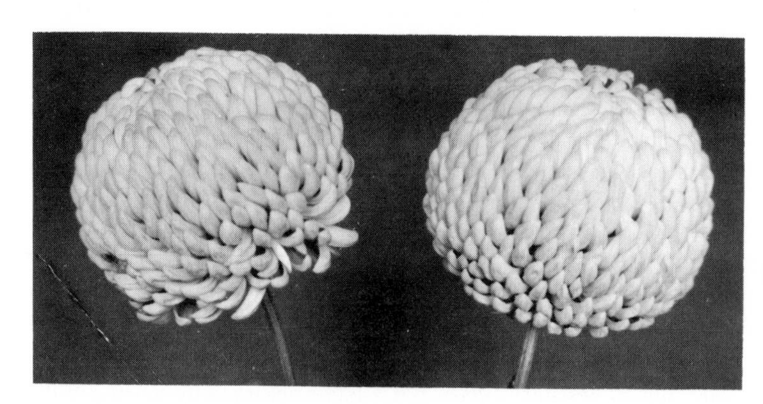

Figure 13.3 Incurves – the Bloom on the Left is Loose and Untidy at the Base

An even and balanced bloom centre is essential. Rough or elongated centres detract from the exhibit. The careful turning over of untidy florets surrounding the central button should be an automatic part of dressing shouldered reflexes. Remove fading basal florets and any which are damping or damaged; a judge always looks underneath. Incurves should be perfectly spherical, and where untidy basal florets give a skirted appearance they should be removed.

Having finished work on the blooms, examine the foliage. Leaves should be clean and free of pests and diseases. The occasional badly scarred leaf is best removed. Dirty leaves or those marked with insecticide powder should be cleaned carefully with a soft cloth and warm water or with a proprietary "leaf shine" product.

With advanced dressing complete, check that all materials are at hand for the following day.

Up Early On The Day

Up early is the order for show day. Allow ample time for packing, travelling, unpacking and staging. The whole season's work can be ruined by undue haste.

There are many ways of getting blooms to the show, varying from the simple bunch for local shows to massive boxes used by some exhibitors for the main events. Alternatively, they can be transported in drums or on racks in hatch-back cars with the stems in small plastic tubes of water. The object is simple: to get them to the show in good condition, and this means that blooms must be secured with no chance of rubbing against their neighbours.

On arrival at the hall select a secluded corner, fill your vases and proceed steadily and methodically. Stage just as in practice, vase by vase, examining each bloom carefully and finally preparing it before putting it into position in its vase. Ensure that the blooms are nicely spaced and standing at the correct height for their position in the vase. This is important and deserves full consideration. On completion check for overall defects, make sure that packing is not visible, endeavour to have leaves spilling nicely over the top of the vase, then wipe the vase with a duster. As each vase is complete stand it in such a position that it cannot be damaged.

Large exhibition and some medium exhibition blooms may take longer to prepare. In addition to any bloom dressing, duplicate foliage will be fitted in the majority of cases and supporting rings may be used to balance the bloom. Any rings should be fitted and adjusted before substitute foliage is added.

On completing the last vase inspect them all carefully again and check that each is entered according to schedule. In the event of an erroneous entry consult the show secretary.

Where a class is for several vases the back ones are displayed more effectively if they are set on 4-in blocks. But blocks should be neat and unobtrusive, preferably green or black in colour. Do not spoil your exhibit and the exhibition by standing vases on unsightly oddments.

Be A Good Loser

When the time comes for checking the awards be a sporting loser. It is so easy to be a good winner, but so much more difficult if you appear to have been harshly treated. Try to be impartial when studying the exhibits and forget the names on the exhibitor's cards. Note carefully why your blooms failed and if necessary seek the advice of more experienced growers or the judge. Listen to what others have to say. Do not swallow it all on the spot, but store it carefully and think about it later.

In the case of the "National" and the larger provincial shows the standard is extremely high and it is no disgrace to have your entry passed by. Many a true top-grade exhibit fails to get an award. All the exhibitor can do is ensure that each exhibit is worthy, then leave the rest to fate and the judges.

In strong competition the exhibitor fortunate enough to be able to grow a large number of plants of each variety does, of course, stand a better chance of securing a matched vase of top-grade blooms on the day, but this will not deter the small grower who exhibits in the right spirit. Many a National champion has come from a small stable.

And when the show is over do not forget the officials. Most of them have no active interest in the show tables and are working unpaid and unsung. But for them there would be no show. So go out of your way to thank them – even after a bad day.

CHAPTER 14

Cut Blooms for Home Decoration

Most chrysanthemums end their days in a vase. This is not surprising, for there are few better cut flowers. Chrysanthemums will last for weeks under cool conditions.

But to get the best out of such long-lasting blooms they must be given assistance. It is not sufficient to put them in a vase and forget them, for the ends of their stems will be exposed to the activities of water-borne bacteria, which gradually block the conductive channels and reduce water uptake. In addition, stems become slimy and the water begins to smell. This is of no consequence with flowers which last for only a few days, but it can drastically reduce the decorative life of chrysanthemums.

It is common practice to cut away the lower clogged portions of the stems at regular intervals to maintain water uptake, and to prevent odour by frequently changing the water, but such operations are tedious and the blooms gradually sink lower and lower in their container. Decorative arrangement is quickly destroyed.

Sugar And Disinfectant Helps

The shortening of stems and the changing of water can be dispensed with, however, if the offending bacteria is destroyed, and this is readily achieved by adding household disinfectant. Furthermore, if sugar is added to the water it helps to ensure that blooms receive the materials they need for the preservation of their qualities. The disinfectant also prevents the formation of slime, and a month later there should be no unpleasant smell.

But the condition of blooms after such a period varies. Some varieties are better keepers than others, and those which are cut younger and fresher and kept cool will last longest.

The additives recommended are a heaped tablespoon of sugar and six drops of disinfectant per pint of water. It will then only be necessary to top up with clear water as the level falls. Proprietary products are also available for this purpose.

Cut Blooms for Home Decoration

Consideration Pays

Blooms cut for decorative purposes should be afforded the same consideration as those for exhibition, though they are not prepared as meticulously.

Cut them a little younger than is normal for exhibition – at about three-quarters developed. Remove foliage to water level and crush the ends of the stems to assist water uptake. Deep water is not an absolute necessity; chrysanthemums last quite well in no more than 2 in, but shallow containers need constant topping up and a depth of 6 to 10 in is more manageable. Stir the "prepared" water thoroughly before inserting the stems.

Arrangement

Arrangement is a complex subject and beyond the scope of these notes, but briefly:

Specimen blooms are at their best in exhibition-style arrangements or variations of this style, or in modern arrangements requiring only a few blooms. Very large blooms are out of place in mixed displays featuring autumn foliage, grasses, berries and fruit. They destroy the effect of lightness so essential to such arrangements. This is the province of the smaller bloom. Small blooms blend into arrangements of almost any shape and size, and are, in fact, highly esteemed by the floral artist.

Evergreens – frequently the only dressing material available – do not always combine with chrysanthemums. The overall effect is often too heavy, though partial plucking of the evergreen sometimes helps. Modern arrangements featuring only a few blooms are most likely to succeed with such heavy dressing material.

First-Aid To Early "Flaggers"

In spite of careful preparation, hard stems occasionally take up insufficient water to keep blooms turgid and after a few days florets become limp. Remove flagging blooms from the vase, stand the ends of the stems in an inch or two of boiling water and leave until it cools. This forces water up the stems and should freshen the bloom. A drastic alternative favoured by some floral artists is to char the bottom inch of stem in a flame, but if blooms are already flagging they would still need the hot water. In fact some exhibitors go so far as to boil water and insert their stems in it for several minutes just prior to staging to make quite sure that their blooms will be fresh.

CHAPTER 15

Special Treatments

Although cultivation is basically the same for all chrysanthemums, some types require special treatment. Some may be raised from seed, though results will always be unpredictable; others require special stopping and training, and so on. A number lend themselves to individual expression in shape and methods of training, and it is perhaps surprising that they are not more popular. A determined and influential grower could well succeed in evolving new fashions in this branch of chrysanthemum decoration.

Charms

Seed can be sown in gentle heat in January, but where selected varieties are to be grown cuttings should be taken, also in January.

As soon as plants are large enough plant into 3½-in pots. Stop at the third or fourth leaf. No further stopping is required. Pot on into 5-in, and then into 8-in to 10-in finals. After planting into finals insert eight to ten split bamboo canes, with a view to the plant growing round them, and as a result becoming virtually self-supporting without the need of ties. Other split canes can be added later.

Choose a well-sheltered standing ground and commence feeding some five weeks after final potting. As plants become larger and begin to spill over the pot it will be necessary to resort to liquid feeds and these should build up in frequency until the plant is being given continual half-strength liquid feeds instead of clear water. Watering-cum-feeding will then be needed daily, and feeding should continue through flowering to maturity. Each plant should be given a quarter-turn every day to ensure symmetrical development.

A cool greenhouse will be sufficient for flowering in mild districts, but heat should be provided in near-frost conditions. Free ventilation should be applied, and if mildew is troublesome a fungicide fumigant should be used.

Smaller plants useful for house decoration may be produced by sowing seed or taking cuttings in late March and potting on to 6 in pots.

An early-flowering form is in existence but seldom seen. It should be treated in the early stages exactly as its late-flowering counterpart, then planted into its flowering position in the garden in mid-May. Allow 2 ft or a little more space between plants.

Cascades

May again be purchased as cuttings in named varieties or propagated from seed. Cuttings are taken or seed sown in January. Pot on as charms. Similar feeding. Plants may be trained in a number of ways:

Cascades
When plants are a few inches high reduce to one or two leading shoots. Final pots must be stood in a sheltered position on a shelf or in a trough 4 or 5 ft above the ground, facing south and protected behind a wall or close screen.

To a short stake inserted in the pot secure a cane pointing downward at an angle near to the perpendicular, and tie the lower end of this cane to a stake driven into the ground. Leading growths are trained down the canes as development proceeds. Tie every few days while the young stems are still pliable. Laterals are stopped every two or three leaves to ensure bushy growth. A length of between 4 ft and 6 ft should be attained.

At housing time the canes are removed and the plants carefully transferred to pedestals or shelves in the greenhouse. Extreme care must be taken in handling.

Pillars
Cascades may also be grown in pillar form by restricting the plant to one or two leaders trained up a stout 5 or 6 ft cane, stopping the laterals every two or three leaves. Culture is otherwise as for the cascade form.

Standards
Another variation is produced by denuding the first two or three feet of the main stem of the pillar form, leaving a bare "trunk", then training a number of laterals over an umbrella-shaped framework. Careful stopping and spacing of growths is necessary to produce a symmetrical domed head of blooms.

Espaliers
This form is produced by planting two plants in one pot, applying an early stop and fanning out the resultant laterals in the fashion of a peacock's tail, securing them to evenly spaced canes thrust into the pot at graduated angles. The leaders are allowed to develop, but

sidegrowths are stopped at every two or three leaves to create the desired pattern.

Standards

Taller-growing small-bloomed chrysanthemums with pliable growth may be trained as standards in the same way as standard cascades. They are given a central stake and grown with or without the wire framework, and trained to produce a symmetrical head of blooms.

Specimen Plants

Exhibition disbud varieties may be grown as shapely specimen plants with upward of a dozen blooms, but the very best specimen plants carry more than a hundred.

The cultivation of large specimens, reaching 4 or 5 ft in diameter is somewhat exacting. Only dedicated growers with the necessary free time can be expected to produce the best examples of these giants. A greenhouse with a wide doorway is also essential.

Select varieties of vigour with pliable growth and where double-flowered varieties are to be used choose varieties with blooms of substance (to avoid open centres). Take cuttings in late November or December. Pot up into 3½-in pots, then successively into 5-in, 9-in, then 18-in. At the final potting the 9-in pot may need to be broken away from the soil ball, for at this stage the plant will be too big to knock from its pot in the normal way without risk of damage. Stop as soon as growths are 6 in to 9 in long, up to four times, the last stop being applied in mid-July.

A single stake is sufficient to begin with, but, as development proceeds, more and more canes will be needed. Then, at the time of the last stop all but six, spaced evenly round the pot, are carefully removed and replaced by a wire "umbrella". Growths must be tied in at frequent intervals with a view to the even spacing of blooms, and plants should be turned a quarter turn every day to ensure even development. An open position well sheltered from winds is essential. Growth retardants can be used to keep growth compact.

Plants must never be allowed to dry out. They are prodigious drinkers and can require anything up to four waterings per day in hot weather. Begin feeding when established in the final pot, but bear in mind that such large plants will need a more generous diet than plants in smaller pots.

Top dressings should be applied in similar fashion to those outlined for conventional disbuds. Disbudding is carried out in the usual way to provide for one bloom at the tip of each final growth.

Dwarf Pot Plants

Naturally dwarf varieties of all chrysanthemums may be grown as single flowered or multi-flowered plants in 6 in or larger pots with pleasing results.

Cuttings are usually taken between late March and the end of May. After rooting pot up into 3½-in, then pot on into finals for flowering. Composts are as for other types in pots of similar size. Stop early, even if this is while the plants are still in small pots for multi-flowered, but allow single-flowered to run up and form a bud. Plants which are to produce one bloom should be sprayed with a growth retarding hormone soon after rooting and again a few weeks later.

Watering is, of course, more frequent with small pots, but plunging the pots up to the rim in moist peat or ashes will keep it down to a reasonable minimum. Feed weekly. If liquids are used give the equivalent of a normal watering at the same strength of feed given to larger pots. If powders are used apply half the amount.

Your nurseryman will be able to suggest suitable varieties. Nurserymen themselves utilise taller varieties and keep them dwarf by chemical means or by daylight control to produce the wonderful dwarf "pot mums" that are seen in florists' shops at all times of the year, but this is a subject demanding study, and the amateur is better advised to begin with naturally dwarf varieties.

Note – Two plants per pot will make for a more bushy effect.

Sprays

Both early-flowering and late-flowering sprays are deservedly popular for *in situ* decoration, as cut flowers and for exhibition. Early-flowering sprays are normally rooted in February, planted out in May, with a stop applied at the end of May or early in June. General cultivation is as for early-flowering disbuds. Feeding should only be necessary where the soil is in poor condition. Allow four to six laterals to each plant. One of the advantages of outdoor sprays is that not only do they provide magnificent bowls of flowers, but they can be grown without any form of protection during flowering.

Late-flowering sprays are a little more demanding, but perhaps even more rewarding in that they can be grown to produce 20 or more blooms to the stem. Another advantage is that they require only a short season of growth, cuttings being inserted in June or July for flowering in November. Where plants are rooted in the middle of June they should be potted into 3½ in and then into 7-in pots of John Innes No. 3 or soilless compost and stopped during the last week of July to produce three flowering laterals. Such methods are calculated to provide beautiful pots of sprays, and if two plants are put in the pot even better effects are produced for home decoration.

But the exhibitor is better advised to leave the insertion of his cuttings until mid-July, potting into 3½ in after rooting and finally into 7 in, allowing plants to run up as a single stem. This method, with only one stem to the pot, provides for better all-round development.

Late-flowering sprays are at their very best when they are "blacked out" for a period. This has the effect of inducing flowering on more of the lower laterals emerging from the main stem, to give a greater number of blooms and greater depth to the spray. Blacking out can be effected by the use of black polythene rolled over a wooden framework. It should be rolled over the plants at approximately 6 pm and removed at approximately 7 am each day from mid-August for a period of approximately six weeks. This may sound somewhat demanding, but in our experience once the necessary arrangements have been made covering and uncovering takes only a few minutes, and the results can be quite breathtaking. Where a thermostatically-controlled fan heater can be positioned under the blackout and set at 60°F even more flowers will be produced on a spray. Blacking out should not continue beyond the point where the bud covering scales begin to break.

Bonsai

While we have experimented with bonsai chrysanthemums, we do not regard ourselves as expert in this branch of chrysanthemum cultivation, and lean on the teachings of our good friend Joe Millett, of California.

Bonsai chrysanthemums are of Japanese origin, being very dwarf, small-leaved and with small flowers. They can be grown in a wide range of styles, and therefore lend themselves to individual expression. Cuttings are taken toward the end of the year or in January, and grown on through successive pottings in the manner of all chrysanthemums, but with special attention to stopping and the training of growths. The first stop is usually made about mid-March, and subsequently other stops are applied every three to four weeks, removing only the tiniest part of the growing tip. Any large leaves are removed. The training of "branches" is achieved by the use of small-gauge copper wire. Do not overwater, overfeed or shade the plants.

Plants are repotted every four to six weeks, and are finally planted into a decorative "show pot", which can be a relatively shallow container, pruning the roots to make this possible.

In order to induce uniform bloom development secondary

growths associated with the basal one-third of the main stem are pinched to two leaves early in September, from the centre one-third five days later, and from the topmost one-third a further five days later. The plant is now kept on the dry side and in full sun to prevent undue elongation of the flowering stems; unwanted growth is pruned away and each bud cluster is disbudded to one bud. Retain buds of even size and aim at the uniform spacing of buds over the entire plant.

Christmas Flowering

Chrysanthemums are understandably popular at Christmas, and most amateurs with a greenhouse decide at some time or other to grow a few plants to decorate the home during the festive season or to pass on to friends.

There are two problems – the choosing of suitable varieties and timing. Not all varieties are suited to Christmas flowering and those that are may not be readily available. Have a chat with your specialist chrysanthemum nurseryman to see what he can offer. Precise timing for Christmas is indeed difficult and, again, seek the advice of your plant supplier concerning potting and stopping dates.

Broadly speaking, cuttings should be inserted in early June, with a stop in mid-July. A 9-in pot of John Innes No. 3 or soilless compost is recommended, with a standard feed or cultural pattern, cropping at four blooms to the plant.

CHAPTER 16

Troubles – and Cures

Every grower faces problems from time to time, and the newcomer may find that a ready reference to some of the main troubles may be helpful.

Stools

Tight clusters of stunted growths – Leafy Gall (a bacterial disease). Destroy stools. Do not use apparently suitable growths springing from the mass of knuckled shoots.
Stools shoots nibbled – Slugs or snails. Put down slug bait.

Young Plants

Mottled foliage – Invariably due to virus diseases. Destroy, and grow on only healthy plants.
"Speckled" foliage and withering lower leaves – Caused by checks due to hasty hardening. More likely where growth has become excessively soft. Plants will grow out of it, but where others are unaffected grow them on in preference.
Reddened lower leaves when hardening – Low temperatures, especially cold winds.
Distorted foliage at shoot tips – Probably aphids. Spray with insecticide.

Mid-Season

White tunnelling on leaves – Chrysanthemum leaf miner grubs. Crush the grubs with the thumbnail and spray weekly from here on with insecticide to control the adult flies.
Yellowing of foliage – Where confined to the lower leaves can be due to magnesium deficiency; where confined to the upper leaves, iron deficiency; where the whole plant appears pale and yellowy the cause could well be waterlogging. In the case of magnesium and iron deficiency apply sequestrene; where waterlogging is suspected allow plants to dry out before more water is applied.
Brown or black triangular patches bounded by the veins and spreading upward – Eelworm. Destroy plants. Existing remedies are not

always convenient to the amateur and the pest will persist and may spread.

Yellowing and withering of foliage, spreading rapidly up the plant in the form of patches but not V-shaped and bounded by the veins – Verticillium Wilt. Destroy affected plants. No practicable cure. In the case of earlies soak the crater from which the plant has been removed with a strong Jeyes or some other disinfectant solution.

Small leaflets in growing tips webbed together – Tiny caterpillars of tortrix moth. Carefully unfold leaflets and destroy caterpillars. Spray into shoot tips with caterpillar specific.

Blind shoots – Capsid bugs, or damage by spray or frost. Capsids are green or brown insects about a quarter of an inch in length, active and with a tendency to hide behind the upper stem as one approaches. Destroy by hand if possible, otherwise powder the shoot tips weekly until buds are well developed. Blindness can also be caused by frosting.

Vertical slits in stems beneath growing tips or buds – Capsid damage. See above. Slit the stem vertically opposite the damage with four or five small vertical slits made with the point of a penknife blade to bring about the straightening of the stem.

Stems splitting horizontally – Excessive rush of sap due to evening watering or heavy rain followed by sudden drop in night temperatures. "Lush growers" are the most susceptible. Pierce the stems right through at 90 degree entry points an inch or two below the growing tip with a thin-bladed penknife to bleed surplus sap. Susceptible pot plants can be provided with polythene "watersheds" over the pots to prevent rain soaking the compost; they should be given only half the normal quantity of water.

Light powdery deposit on foliage – Mildew. From the time of first appearance spray fortnightly with an appropriate fungicide.

Buds

Buds heeling over (no scar present) – In the main a varietal defect. Can be corrected by vertical slits on the outer bend of the stem (as for capsid damage) or the stem can be strapped to a split bamboo flower stick with electrical adhesive tape while it is still soft and pliable.

Buds damaged – Caterpillars, earwigs or capsids. Handpicking and routine sprays.

Blooms

Buds rotting – Overfeeding. Decide on a lighter diet to the offending variety next year.

Buds and large central areas of blooms rotting – Ray Blight. Remove and destroy affected blooms, trim the plant for cuttings production and spray thoroughly with a captan or maneb product or some other suitable fungicide.

Damping of blooms (black rotting spots and patches on florets) – Some varieties susceptible to the defect. Intensified where plants were overfed. Can be due to a humid atmosphere leading to invasion of chrysanthemum Petal Spot or Botrytis spores. Endeavour to keep humidity down to a reasonable level.

Florets nibbled and holed; black specks of insect frass present – Earwigs or caterpillars. Handpicking, plus spraying with insecticides.

Occasional malformed blooms, with some florets shorter than the rest, sometimes with a wedge-shaped portion failing to develop – Probably capsid bug, but could be earwig damage in the bud stage. Handpicking, routine sprays.

All blooms on a plant malformed, with rolled, twisted florets and generally ragged appearance – Aspermy Virus. Burn affected plants.

Reflexes tending to incurve – Can be due to a rich diet, to early buds developing in long days, to undercropping or to high temperatures during flowering.

Incurving varieties tending to reflex – Most usually caused by low temperatures during flowering.

Elliptical centres – Usually a varietal failing. Can be "masked" to some degree by increased cropping, but this does not remove the basic defect.

"Pinking" of lower florets – Caused by low temperatures. Double bag susceptible white and yellow earlies; keep night temperatures at 50-55°F in the greenhouse.

Decay of lower florets before the blooms are fully developed – Can be a varietal failing, but intensified by a too generous diet and/or flagging due to dryness at the roots, especially in sunshine. More likely where root action is defective.

Poor colour – Can be due to nutrient deficiency such as magnesium, iron or potassium, but more likely to be due to high temperatures during bud formation and flowering.

"Daisy-eye" (open centre) – A weakness with some varieties; intensified where the stop is applied too late and buds develop late in the season under shortening days.

Generally coarse blooms – Due to excessive nutrition, to carrying too few blooms to the plant. More likely on early buds.

Detailed information on pests and diseases of chrysanthemums is available in the British National Chrysanthemum Society's publication *Pests, Diseases and Nutritional Disorders of Chrysanthemums* by Dr Nigel Scopes.

CHAPTER 17

A Calendar Guide

It is impossible to establish a calendar guide for chrysanthemum cultivation which applies in every season to every grower, and the following pages are simply intended to remind the newcomer of successive routine operations. Dates given are those which would normally apply in the southern half of Britain, and the necessary amendments should be made for other localities, for extreme weather conditions and to cater for varying personal outlooks. A six months ajustment will be needed in the Southern Hemisphere.

January

First Week

Study the month's cuttings programme.

Where stock is being wintered throughout in the cold frame check for the presence of slugs and renew slug bait as necessary. But where a greenhouse is in use boxed stools should now be transferred to the greenhouse staging with a view to keeping them more moist and warmer for more speedy cuttings production.

Remove any coarse or defective stools growths which will obviously be unsuitable for propagation purposes.

Where propagation has not yet commenced assemble the equipment needed and check that adequate stocks of the rooting medium are at hand.

Test the earlies plot for lime needs and apply as necessary (see page 58).

Second Week

Re-read Chapter 3 on "Propagation".

If stools growths required for mid-February rooting are backward apply gentle bottom heat for the next few weeks and consider giving a quick-acting nitrogenous liquid feed.

Insert the main batch of large exhibition and medium exhibition cuttings.

Third Week

Don't overdo the heating and coddle the stools – 35° to 40°F at night is adequate where growths are developing satisfactorily – but remember when ventilating that an icy, dry airflow can be damaging. In hard weather keep the greenhouse all but closed.

Apply a few drops of oil to fan heaters at intervals; keep paraffin lamps clean and wicks trimmed.

Fourth Week

Re-read Chapter 5 on "Potting Up and Hardening".

Insert cuttings of October-flowering varieties to be grown as earlies.

Insert the remainder of large exhibition and medium exhibition cuttings.

Assemble materials in readiness for the first potting of the main batch of large exhibition and medium exhibition blooms.

February

First Week

Study the month's cuttings programme.

Assemble materials for the second potting of December-rooted large and medium exhibition varieties.

Insert cuttings of late flowering incurves, reflexes, intermediates and singles.

Second Week

Where light soils have not yet been prepared they should be dug in the coming weeks.

Insert cuttings of earlies during the next few weeks; also October-flowering varieties required for October flowering.

Keep watch for aphids in shoot tips.

Third Week

Assemble materials for the first potting of February-rooted lates and earlies.

Renew slug bait in the frames.

Wash and sterilise pots and crocks of last year's lates as stools are discarded.

Fourth Week

Newly potted plants should be stood on the cool staging of the greenhouse and watered only when in need. Ventilation should be applied whenever the outside temperature is 40°F or above.

March

First Week

Study the month's cuttings programme.

Check stopping dates and note varieties needing a very early stop.

Insert cuttings of October-flowering varieties to be grown as lates.

Prepare the frames for the hardening phase (see p. 62).

Charms need stopping at the third or fourth leaf.

Second Week

Fork over the earlies plot as soon as the soil is friable.

Assemble materials for the second potting of January-rooted large exhibition and medium exhibition.

Check the store cupboard to ensure that adequate stocks of the following are held for the season's need: slug bait, insecticides, fungicides, insecticide powder, fertilisers, black thread for protecting earlies, tying material, canes, vaseline for anti-earwig operations, bags for bloom protection.

Third Week

When roots have begun to work into the compost of the first pot – say two weeks after potting – plants can be transferred to the frames for hardening.

Check posts and straining wires on the lates standing ground.

Fourth Week

Re-read Chapter 7 on "Stopping and Timing".

Plants received through the post should stand in water for an hour before potting if roots are dry; they should then be positioned in a lightly shaded corner of the greenhouse for ten to fourteen days before transfer to the frames for hardening.

First Week

Peruse the stopping list periodically.

Assemble materials for the second potting of early-rooted earlies and February-rooted late-flowering incurves, reflexes, intermediates and singles.

Commence weekly insecticide sprays in the frames as the weather begins to warm. Keep a special watch for aphids and leaf miners.

If sparrows become troublesome with plants in the frames make use of metal-foil bird scarers.

Second Week

The first stop to most late-flowering singles and second-crown late-flowering incurves is now due.

Apply the base dressing to the earlies plot (see p. 78).

Clean and sterilise pots and boxes as they are discarded, using Jeyes Fluid or some other horticultural disinfectant.

When ventilating the frames tilt the lights in such a way that cold winds are channelled over the plants and do not blow directly on to them.

Third Week

Where a loam stack is to be built obtain turves for stacking in the next few weeks (see p. 48).

If premature buds appear in growing tips nip them out and run on a sideshoot.

Fourth Week

Re-read Chapter 8 on "Planting the Earlies".

Finally plan outdoor stations for earlies and make out a chart of any comparative tests which are to be conducted.

May

First Week

Insert canes in readiness for planting out the earlies (see p. 78).

Assemble materials for the final potting of lates.

Keep a special watch for aphids in shoot tips and keep up the vigil until buds have formed. Inspect tips at least once a week.

Second Week

Well water earlies the day before planting out. Plant out toward the middle of the month (see p. 78).

Prepare the standing ground for lates (see p. 84).

Most earlies should be stopped by the middle of the month to ensure long, strong laterals of full bloom-size potential.

The final potting of lates now gets under way (see p. 81).

Third Week

Re-read Chapter 10 on "The Growing Season".

Try to keep the earlies moving steadily forward after planting out.

Water as necessary in dry spells.

Fourth Week

Stop remaining large and medium exhibition varieties, except where second stops are needed to delay flowering.

When spraying pay particular attention to small laterals developing in the leaf axils. Study them for possible aphid build-ups.

June

First Week

Keep the surface of the earlies plot open and weed-free.

If newly potted lates flag badly they must be watered (see p. 84). Two weeks after potting they can be placed on the standing

ground.
Insert cuttings for Christmas flowering.

Second Week
Be on guard for leaf miners, capsid bugs and earwigs from now on.
The second stop to most late-flowering singles and second-crown incurves is now due.
Continue with lateral countdown to crop plus one spare.
Insert cuttings of late-flowering sprays to be stopped for flowering at three sprays to the plant.

Third Week
Basal shoots will soon begin to appear. Don't pull them up indiscriminately, but nip them off carefully at ground level. The tops could be rooted to increase stock.
Commence routine feeds to lates four or five weeks after final potting (see p. 91).

Fourth Week
Putty up open cane tops to prevent earwigs residing in them.
Ensure that developing laterals are well supported to avoid loss in high winds.
Turn charms and specimen plants a quarter-turn each day to ensure balanced all-round development.

July

First Week
Re-read Chapter 7 on "Stopping and Timing".
Buds of earlies will soon begin to appear. If several weeks too soon consider "run-by" treatment (see p. 76-7).
Don't water until a plant is in need, but avoid severe flagging, especially after buds appear.

Second Week
Re-read Chapter 11 on "Flowering the Earlies".
Keep the notebook columns up to date.
The final stop to most Christmas-flowering varieties is now due.
Watch for mildew on lower leaves and spray every two weeks with a mildew specific from when it first appears.
Insert cuttings of late-flowering sprays to be grown straight up without stopping.

Third Week
The disbudding of earlies will now be well under way. Remove unwanted growths at the earliest possible moment.

Withering lower leaves should be removed.
Prepare for the final staking and protection of earlies.

Fourth Week
Stop June-rooted late-flowering sprays to produce three laterals.
Paint and overhaul the greenhouse and frames – don't leave it to a last minute scramble at the end of the season.
Erect covers over earlies at calyx break to colour show (see p. 105).

August

First Week
Stake earlies firmly and well up to the buds.
Except where blooms are bagged, apply a ring of vaseline round the upper stems to deter earwigs.
Secure buds of large exhibition and medium exhibition varieties in the next week or two.

Second Week
Re-read Chapter 13 on "Exhibition".

Third Week
Check planned exhibition dates and assemble necessary equipment. Re-check classifications.

Fourth Week
Re-read Chapter 12 on "Flowering Lates".
Where large exhibition varieties are concerned it is time to think about preparing the greenhouse.
Buds of late-flowering incurves, reflexes and intermediates should be secured in the next few weeks.
Keep watch for earwigs in opening blooms of earlies. See that they are securely staked and properly protected.

September

First Week
Don't forget white oil sprays to the foliage of earlies needed for exhibition.
Check the greenhouse heating equipment.
Large and medium exhibition varieties will need housing between calyx break and colour show (see p. 111), though some growers bag the buds and leave them out until later in the month for stems to ripen thoroughly.

Second Week
Re-read Chapter 16 on "Troubles – and Cures".

Watch for good and bad plants of earlies; also for new varieties of merit. Keep the plot tidy as the blooms come and go.

Secure the buds of late-flowering singles in the next two or three weeks.

Bear in mind the possibility of feeds during bloom development (see p. 108).

Third Week

Most lates are housed in the second half of the month in southern Britain. But leave Christmas-flowering plants outside until frosts make housing necessary.

Fourth Week

Now is the time to plan next season's earlies – while this year's results are still fresh in the mind.

Continue with routine sprays to earlies, even after the blooms have been cut; keep watch for slugs attacking stools growths.

Maintain a steady air circulation in the greenhouse, keep the atmosphere on the dry side and water with a half-pint per pot when the surface of the compost begins to dry.

October

First Week

Re-read Chapter 4 on "Composts and Soils".

Prepare for bedding earlies stools.

Remove any damping florets on lates as they appear and dress unruly florets into position.

Turn pots of late-flowering singles and sprays a quarter-turn each day to ensure balanced development.

Second Week

Re-read Chapter 2 on "Wintering Stools and Buying Plants".

Third Week

Watch for pests in developing blooms of lates – earwigs in particular.

Fourth Week

Re-read Chapter 13 on "Exhibition".

Keep basal growths of lates trimmed according to the date required for the variety (see p. 28).

Watch for good and bad plants of lates; also for new varieties of merit. Keep the notebook up to date.

November

First Week
Re-read Chapter 1 on "The Real Beginning".
Lift and box or bed stools of earlies (see p. 28).

Second Week
After flowering cut down stems of lates to a foot or so and remove the old foliage.

Third Week
Browse over Chapter 18 "A Deeper Insight".
Complete next season's plans and decide on any cultural changes.
Order new varieties for next season.
Fit polythene lining in the greenhouse in the coming weeks.

Fourth Week
Re-read Chapter 2 on "Wintering Stools and Buying Plants".
Assemble propagation equipment where December-rooting is planned.

December

First Week
Clean, repair and sterilise tools and equipment.
Check stocks of canes, pots, labels, lime and peat.

Second Week
Re-read Chapter 4 on "Composts and Soils".
Check advanced stools for potential cuttings and remove obviously unsuitable growths.
Insert cuttings of large exhibition varieties needing a very early start in the next few weeks.

Third Week
Prepare the greenhouse for any boxed or potted stools to be transferred from the frames.

Fourth Week
Clean the greenhouse glass.
If soilborne pests, such as springtails and woodlice appear on the surface of stools compost, resort to insecticide powder.
Assemble materials for the first potting of December-rooted large exhibition varieties.
Reflect on the season past and plan for even better things next year!

CHAPTER 18

A Deeper Insight

This chapter is intended for those who desire further insight into the functions of the plant, with a view to more complete mastery of the art of cultivation. The mastery of any art demands skill and in many cases exceptional ability: in the case of the chrysanthemum anything approaching complete mastery requires some understanding of its inner workings. This is not a deep and mysterious study, and in the following pages we shall be looking mainly to facts based on scientific discovery and to the results of personal observations and experiments rather than indulging in theory – though deduction must play its part, since all that we would like to know is not yet known.

The section on bloom form has not been covered in detail in any published work of our acquaintance, and time may point to flaws in our assessments, but we believe that our detailed principles will be of interest and value to keen plantsmen.

Appreciation of the beauty of flowers is based on the characteristics of their florets (or petals), their colour and form. In other than single chrysanthemums, size of bloom is dependent on the number of florets it contains and on the size of those florets; colour is dependent on pigments; bloom form is dependent on the final shape and arrangement of the florets. One must be mindful, too, that while a bloom is made up of its florets, a floret is made up of countless tiny cells, and the constitution of these cells largely determines bloom quality. Therefore, it is logical that you should know something about both cells and florets.

Perhaps the best way to arrive at co-ordinated understanding is to look in turn at the desired bloom qualities, size, colour, form and freshness, together with two factors which can reduce quality, namely "pinking" and damping, ending with a brief look at foliage in its role as a pleasing backcloth to the blooms.

Some of the content of this chapter is a repeat of what has been stated earlier, but of necessity for the intention is to now portray bloom development and factors affecting bloom quality more compactly in such a way that those who so desire can make use of the separate items for purposes of revision.

Size

We saw in earlier chapters that bloom size is influenced by lateral size, that a larger receptacle with more florets will result not only from extra lateral vigour but also from bud development taking place under long days of good light. We saw, too, that florets are formed during the bud swell period as a result of cells "dividing" and multiplying, one cell becoming two cells and so on. We should again bear in mind that it is only in this period that cells increase in numbers, and where growth is reasonably vigorous and the rate of cell division is appreciable florets will develop with more cells and with considerable floret and bloom size potential. Where laterals have developed in the form of a long-V, with leaves becoming larger as they ascend the stem, the vigour enjoyed in the topmost leaves will also influence development within the bud.

Plant hormones called "kinins" stimulate cell division, and kinins are synthesised in developing roots and translocated to regions of growth; it is therefore desirable that there is a developing root system during bud swell, a situation which is automatically provided for in the open soil. In the case of pot plants the need can be covered to some degree by providing compost top dressings (see p. 100). It is preferable to contrive to keep roots extending gently in a mildly nutritive medium rather than applying heavier feeding to a virtually dormant root system.

While the *number* of embryo cells formed in young florets in the bud may be important, their *constitution* is equally so, for after their formation by cell division they have a further function to fulfil, their final expansion when the bloom unfolds, and their early constitution will have a bearing on the extent of this expansion.

Tiny cells are at first completely filled with protoplasm, the "living substance" of the plant, made up in the main of proteins, which we could regard as being composed of water, sugar derivatives and nitrogen, plus sulphur and in some cases phosphorus. Practically, it could be said that where nitrogen is in ample supply sugars are in effect commandeered for protein synthesis, so reducing sugar concentrations. But where nitrogen is in reduced supply embryo floret cells will be reduced in protein content, and it is conceivable that they will contain extra sugar-based materials which will later be utilised for increased cell expansion (referred to as "vacuolation"). In fact it is suggested that stored sugar derivatives in cells are converted to "active" sugar at the commencement of vacuolation by the hormone auxin, to fulfil their vital roles in cell expansion and the development of the floret and bloom. This brings us back to the need of balanced condition. We should also bear in mind that high night temperatures after the bud becomes visible can adversely affect bloom size. The ideal is in the region of 50°F.

After its initiation a bud will grow relatively slowly over a period of several weeks, building up its florets, their quota of cells and their protoplasm, until it reaches the point where its protective tissues begin to split. "Calyx break", as it is called, heralds the beginning of the final phase of floret development. Although in large blooms with many florets cell division may still be proceeding at the centre of the bloom, the cells of the first outer florets, having completed their period of cell division, will now be on the verge of relatively dramatic expansion, the first visual signs of which can be noticed as florets become tipped with the colour of the bloom. It is vacuolation, the "blowing up" of cells rather like the inflation of so many balloons, which finally enlarges the floret and produces the bloom.

When one reflects on the relatively lengthy period between the formation of the first floret cells and the commencement of cell expansion, the onset of vacuolation is relatively sudden, as if triggered by some hidden control, and it operates at virtually the same time in all the cells of a floret, obviously under the influence of some co-ordinating factor. In fact, a plant exercises many such controls, in a way which is, as yet, far beyond human understanding.

If we further consider the needs of an individual floret cell during the period of bloom opening we shall be considering the needs of the entire floret and the entire bloom.

The commencement of vacuolation is said to be accompanied by the sudden appearance in the protoplasm of the cell of concentrations of sugars, and at the same time tiny areas of watery solution begin to develop. They later coalesce to form one large central "vacuole", with the protoplasm receding to line the cell wall.

The "sudden appearance" of sugars in the cell at the commencement of vacuolation does, in fact, point to the possibility of conversion of sugar derivatives already in the cell into an active form, for sugars have an important part to play in vacuolation, and intake tests with staining dyes show no veinal intake by the young floret in the early stages of vacuolation. If this is so, cells need to accumulate and store sugars in some form during the bud swell period, and leaves have to be in the necessary condition to supply them. Also, if there is conversion of "stored" materials, then there must be an agent of conversion; there is evidence to suggest that auxin could be the important agent. At the same time auxin makes the cell wall plastic and suitable for extension, and possibly more suitable for the intake of external supplies of vacuolative materials. We know for certain that sugars appear; that vacuoles develop and water is drawn in; that the cell wall becomes conditioned for extension. We also know that there is a relatively considerable need of sugars in the bloom-opening period and that excessive feeding up to the bud and/or during the bud can reduce bloom size.

A vacuolating cell needs water, nutrients, growth hormones and sugars.

Water is needed to fill the enlarging watery vacuole, and fortunately the need is readily met by keeping the roots reasonably well supplied.

Growth-activating nutrients are also needed, especially nitrogen, which is said to have the effect of making the cell wall more "elastic" and therefore more subject to extension; experiments have shown that quick-acting nutrients in the form of "bloom feeds" can lead to larger floret cells (see p. 108). While the cells of florets produced on an excessive diet in the pre-bud or bud periods can be so composed that full expansion during bloom opening is not possible, if a plant has been produced in balanced condition and cells have a reasonable content of sugar derivatives then quick-acting liquid feeds during bloom opening will ensure that any sugars the floret cells contain or take in will be fully utilised.

Growth hormones, auxin and gibberellin, and possibly others, are needed by the cell during vacuolation. Cells will be larger where they are in full supply. Practically, we can regard growth hormone requirements as being fully catered for where nutrition is adequate, where daylength and daylight are of sufficient duration and intensity, and where roots are still gently active. Auxin is produced in developing tissues and is most likely to be in full supply where nutrition is adequate and growth is vigorous; gibberellin is produced in active roots and translocated to growing points to stimulate cell development.

Last, but by no means least, and in many ways the most tantalising of the requirements, let us consider *sugars*. Sugars and their derivatives are the source of energy for all the processes of cell extension; they provide the basic materials for the growth of the cell wall, and in solution in the watery content of the central vacuole they play an important part in "drawing in" more water by the process of osmosis to ensure the full expansion of the cell, and therefore the full expansion of the floret and bloom.

The initial vacuolative impulse seems to be almost entirely dependent on the utilisation of materials already in the cell, put there in the bud swell period. This is further indicated by the fact that where a plant is completely stripped of its leaves at colour show, blooms still develop, though they are considerably smaller. But as floret extension proceeds and the longitudinal veinal system of the floret, running from the stub to the tip, becomes operative, supplies will be taken in at an increasing rate, and the extent and nature of those supplies will further influence floret development. Ideally, such supplies will contain ample quantities of nutrients, growth hormones and sugars. Sugars will now be delivered direct from the leaves, and obviously where leaves are in condition to export an appreciable percentage of what they manufacture this will further assist floret development. In fact, at this point, with vegetative extension having reached its conclusion most of the products of the leaves are diverted into the developing blooms. Opening blooms are looked upon as "sinks" into which the products of the leaves now pour, and in tests on other subjects flower and fruit size has been found to be relative to the number of leaves supplying each flower and fruit. Back to the dry weight theory! Other tests have confirmed that movement early in the bud to ensure full cell division and full development of the upper leaves is important.

But if temperatures rise, the rate of respiration rises in all living cells, due to an increased rate of metabolic activity; respiration consumes sugars, which means that under high temperatures sugars are depleted and there is less available for floret cell expansion. This will adversely affect colour, and in many cases form, as well as size. We saw earlier that blooms can be smaller where the night temperature is 60°F as opposed to 50°F during the bud development period. Then when we come to bloom opening, some varieties fail to develop their central florets fully at a night level of 60° as opposed to 50°F. Temperatures may rise by day in sunshine without harmful effect, but night temperatures should not be too high. A night temperature of 60°F is regarded as ideal in the brief period of bud initiation, but 50°F is more favourable after the buds are visible and during flowering, with a rise of 10° or so by day. But these ideals, desirable though they may be, are seldom attainable.

So the requirements of bloom size can be clearly defined. We need:

(a) long, strong laterals of full leaf count, with buds developing in long days of good light;

(b) sufficient vigour of growth during the period of bud swell to ensure full cell division in the developing florets, with full expansion of the upper leaves, yet with the plant in balanced condition;

(c) full vacuolation of the floret cells during the period of bloom opening.

With such understanding, when results fall short of the ideal adjustments can be made which are calculated to correct the deficiency and the cultural routine can be modified accordingly.

Colour

Our perception and enjoyment of colour is due to the fact that light consists of a range of colour bands (or "light waves") running from violet, through blue, green, yellow and orange to red, with (perhaps surprisingly) their combined effect producing white. Basically we can look upon light as consisting of blue, red and yellow colour bands; if an object absorbs only the blue and yellow bands the red band will be reflected back and the eye will see that object as red. If a pigment absorbs red and reflects back blue and yellow the associated object is seen as green.

Florets contain pigments which absorb certain of the colour bands and which reflect the others back to the eye, and it is the type and concentration of these pigments which determines floret and bloom colour.

Chrysanthemum colour is basically fixed in accordance with the inherited characteristics of the variety, and depends on the presence and concentration of two types of colour pigments, red anthocyanin and yellow carotenoids. A third pigment, anthoxanthin, is present in the florets of all chrysanthemums, but it absorbs none of the visible light waves, and in the absence of anthocyanin and carotenoid it reflects back all the light waves and the floret will appear white. In addition chlorophyll can be present in some chrysanthemum florets to impart green colouration.

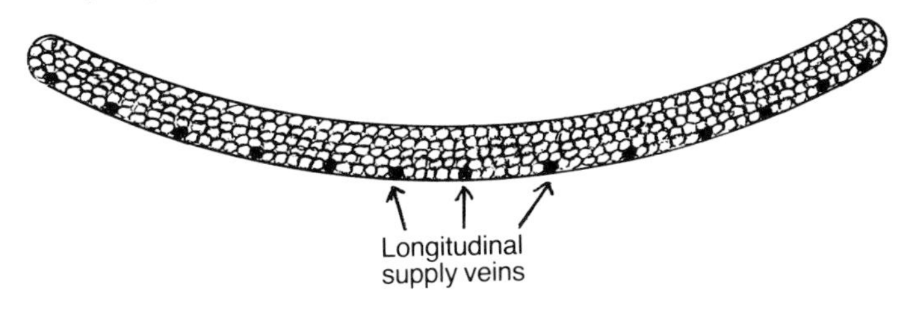

Figure 18.1
Lateral
Cross-section of
Floret

Anthocyanin (red) pigments in upper cell layer only

Carotenoid (yellow) pigments can occur in both upper and lower cell layers, and on occasion in central cell layers

Upper cell layer more responsive to vacuolative expansion than lower cell layer

Marginal tissues more sensitive to vacuolative expansion than central tissues

Chrysanthemum florets can be looked upon as having approximately five layers of cells, an inner (upper) cell layer, an outer (lower) cell layer and a central group of approximately three layers. The inner (upper) cell layer is the only one containing red anthocyanin, but it can also contain yellow carotenoids; the outer (lower) cell layer, and in some cases the central layers, may also contain carotenoids, but not anthocyanin.

Anthocyanins are somewhat unstable sap-soluble pigments located in the central sap-filled vacuole of floret cells. They absorb blue and yellow waves of the visible spectrum and reflect back red waves to the eye. Only one type of anthocyanin has been identified in chrysanthemum floret cells, and colour intensity based on anthocyanin is therefore dependent on pigment concentration and not on the type of pigment. Pale pinks have a low anthocyanin concentration and deep reds have considerably more. Purples contain even greater concentrations. With anthocyanin confined to the inner (upper) cell layer, red and purple colouration is most intense on the inside of the florets of incurving varieties and the outside of reflexes. In company with yellow carotenoids they impart various shades of orange and bronze.

Carotenoids occur in the protoplasm of the cell as insoluble and relatively stable granules. Three distinct types have been identified in chrysanthemum florets; though normally associated with the inner and outer cell layers they can occur in central cell layers. They are all yellow in colour, for they absorb red and blue light waves and reflect the yellow waves back to the eye. Where they occur in company with anthocyanin the colour of the inner (upper) surface of the floret will be red, orange or bronze, depending on the concentrations of anthocyanin and carotenoids present; where they occur in the outer (lower) cell layer the "reverse" of the floret will be yellow, and therefore where the two above examples occur together a red, orange or bronze inner (upper) floret surface with a yellow reverse is produced.

Anthoxanthin pigments have been observed in all chrysanthemums so far examined, but they absorb only ultra-violet light waves, which are invisible to the eye, and they therefore reflect all visible light waves back to the eye and appear white. White varieties contain anthoxanthin, but no anthocyanin or carotenoids; creams contain anthoxanthin and small amounts of carotenoid.

It will therefore be seen that bloom colour in the chrysanthemum is due to:

(a) pink, red and purple – anthocyanins
(b) yellow – carotenoids
(c) white – anthoxanthin

Blends of the above can lead to other colourations and depth of colour depends on the concentration of the pigments.

Practically, whites present us with no problems of colour density or stability, and carotenoids are not only able to form in poor light but they are relatively stable. Anthocyanin is less stable.

In contrast with carotenoids, anthocyanin needs light for its development and where light is poor the concentration of anthocyanin will be reduced. The synthesis of anthocyanin is finally dependent on sugars, and when sugar is in low concentration in florets cells anthocyanin will be reduced in concentration. Therefore, where nitrogen is excessive and the carbon/nitrogen ratio in the plant is low, and where as a result embryo floret cells possess only limited sugar derivatives in their protoplasm, colour shades dependent on anthocyanin are likely to be depleted. Similarly, where temperatures are high during the period of pigment synthesis, respiration will be high, and since respiration consumes sugars less sugar will be available for anthocyanin synthesis. So both excessive nitrogen and high temperatures can reduce colour in pinks, reds, bronzes and purples. Carotenoids are less temperamental. While they form earlier in the life of the cell but only appear in their true colour at the time of vacuolation, they are little affected by the factors which interfere with anthocyanin.

Pinks, red, bronzes and purples can be pale in colour when they develop under heat wave conditions, but if the weather pattern changes, with a sudden drop in temperature, florets developing later on the same bloom will be equally suddenly deeper in colour, to give a bloom with a pale base and a deeply coloured crown, indicating:

(a) that temperature affects colour based on anthocyanin,
(b) that the colour of the floret is finally determined as the floret unfolds,
(c) that once a floret has lost its colour it cannot be restored,
(d) that colour cannot move from floret to floret – in fact it cannot move from cell to cell: pigments are confined to the cells of their origin.

Although colour appears in florets as they open, colour *potential* is influenced in earlier days, by the cultivation technique, by the gradual ripening of tissues, and by so managing the plant that sugar supplies to developing buds and blooms will be adequate, especially in the case of anthocyanin. It is also important to bear in mind that colour can be affected by temperatures during the period of bud development (see p. 102). In short, colour potential is laid down long before the moment of flowering, but is finally determined by conditions at the time of bloom opening. The moment of vacuolation, with its sudden increase in sugar concentration within the cell, is not surprisingly the time of pigment formation and colour development. Similarly, as vacuolative development comes to an end so colour development ceases, and having come to their natural conclusions neither can be reactivated.

All too often it is thought that the answer to colour problems is to apply liberal quantities of iron, potassium or magnesium to the soil. This is seldom the answer. In fact, copious supplies of potassium can reduce the intake of magnesium and reduce colour. Poor colour is far more likely to be due to high temperatures than to nutrient deficiencies.

Both strong light and high temperatures can bleach colour after it has been imparted, by increasing radiant energy to such a level that pigments are chemically decomposed, more especially where anthocyanin is concerned. Again, once colour has been lost it cannot be restored. Shading with butter muslin during bloom development will help to keep temperatures down, but heavy shading will reduce the level of light needed for anthocyanin synthesis.

The ideal temperature, as seen under "Size", is in the region of 50°F by night, with a rise of approximately 10°F during daylight. If temperatures rise well above these levels colour is likely to be reduced.

Form

The form assumed by blooms is basically inherited and natural to the variety, though in some cases it varies according to the weather, cultivation or geographical location.

The florets of virtually all blooms are at first incurving, and some remain incurving under all normal cultural and climatic conditions. Others always change in form as they develop to become reflexing. But there are those which are subject to considerable variation, sometimes incurving, sometimes reflexing, sometimes reflexing at the base of the bloom and incurving at the top, or incurving at the base and reflexing at the top.

Obviously, a particular form is desirable for each variety, depending on its official form classification, and it is therefore in our interests to know what causes different form variations and to know how best to control them.

As we saw under "Colour", a floret consists of three distinct types of cell layer, and it is the different characteristics of these layers, plus the different response of marginal and central floret tissues to the vacuolative impulse, which finally controls floret form, and therefore bloom form.

The inner (upper) cell layer could be looked upon as the most active in terms of vacuolative expansion when the floret unfolds, while the outer (lower) cell layer is more "substantial" in its composition and less responsive to the vacuolative impetus. In other words the inner cell layer tends to expand more than the outer cell layer. The central cell layers can be regarded as somewhat "neutral" in their effect on form, though they obviously need to expand approximately equally to those of the upper and lower cuticular layers.

We saw under "Size", that a floret develops initially in its cell layers by the process of cell division, and at the end of cell division it will contain its full quota of cells, each filled with protoplasm and containing a variable amount of sugar derivatives. We saw that sugar has an influence on floret and bloom size and on colour. We shall further see that it can also have an effect on floret and bloom form.

Vacuolation is triggered universally throughout the floret in such a way that all the cells commence vacuolation at approximately the same time, and the initial expansion of the floret is somewhat uniform, with the floret developing in incurving form.

Virtually all florets are at first incurving, and the intensity of their early development, and to some degree their early form, will be influenced by factors both before and during this phase of development. Extra nutrition either before or during bud swell makes for more "vegetative" development of the floret cells, especially those of the outer (lower) cell layer with its riblike supply lines. This is due in part to resultant increased protein synthesis and reduced sugar deposits in the cells, but it could also be associated with nutrient-induced hormone activation, especially affecting the development of the outer cell layers.

Varieties which tend to be variable in form also have a greater tendency to incurve when buds are early and they develop under long days. Again the cause must be extra vigour of growth in the period of bud development, with extra growth potential in the outer cell layer and in the more central floret tissues relative to marginal tissues.

Another interesting and important consideration is the effect of varying temperature levels, especially night temperatures. We have seen that night temperatures during the period of bud development can affect form, and night temperatures during bloom opening are certainly likely to do so, high temperatures favouring incurving and low temperatures favouring reflexing. Why?

The effect of temperature varies with the variety. Some incurve at virtually all temperature levels, and others always reflex, but some "variables" tend to incurve at a night temperature of 60°F and reflex at 50°F. Furthermore, at the higher level the central florets of some varieties develop in thin, spiky form, whereas at the lower level of 50°F they are considerably broader, longer *and of better colour*, with a greater tendency to turn over into fully reflexing form.

So, lower temperatures not only favour reflexing, but they lead to extra cell and floret size *and to deeper anthocyanin colour*. While hormones may well be involved, the above considerations point to sugar concentrations within the floret cells as being the important final factor, for sugar concentration varies with temperature changes. At low temperatures respiration is low and sugar concentrations are likely to be relatively high, while at high temperatures respiration is high and sugars are depleted. Low temperatures, with their extra sugar concentrations, lead to full anthocyanin colour, to full cell vacuolation and extra floret size, and to a greater tendency to reflexing. High temperatures, with lower sugar concentrations, lead to reduced anthocyanin colouration, to reduced cell vacuolation and reduced floret development, and to a reduced likelihood of a change to reflexing form. The three factors are obviously linked, and sugar concentrations are obviously involved.

A further pointer to the possibility of sugar concentration being an important agent of form changes is the effect of high and low nutrition. Where nutrition is high the carbon/nitrogen ratio will be low – in other words, sugar concentrations will be reduced – and incurving is more likely. Furthermore, incurves tend to have small leaves, and small leaves would be reduced in their sugar-manufacturing capacity, which would mean a low carbon/nitrogen ratio. Again, low sugar concentrations lead to incurving form, with smaller florets and smaller blooms! In fact, incurves do tend to be smaller than reflexes. This does not mean that all incurves and incurving varieties will have small blooms, but it does imply that their florets would be larger if they had the extra vacuolative vigour to make them reflex.

The initial phase of expansion resulting from the activation of materials already in the cells is shortly followed by intensified expansion due to the commencement of the intake of sap-borne supplies of growth-stimulating materials. This intake occurs as a result of the floret seemingly becoming receptive to external supplies as part of the pattern of bloom development. Such supplies were always available, but it is only now that floret tissues become receptive to them, and, conveniently, it is when blooms begin to develop that vegetative extension ceases and all the plant's growth materials are channelled to developing blooms.

Tests with staining dyes have shown up to twelve to sixteen supply veins in a small floret, spaced at intervals across the breadth of the floret and located in the outer (lower) cell layer, running from the stub toward the tip. There are no lateral branching subsidiary veins, as in the case of the leaf.

The veinal pattern of dye intake is by no means uniform for all florets, but this may be due to varying ability to absorb large molecules of dye rather than to any difference in the basic veinal system. In some cases the initial intake of dye appears as a strong flow into a central vein, or into two parallel central veins, with the tissues close to these veins (in the outer cell layer) showing extra development and lengthening relative to more marginal tissues to intensify the incurving form, suggesting extra development in floret tissues close to the intake of new supplies. This initial intake is shortly followed by less pronounced intake by other smaller veins spread across the floret – at least this is the evidence of our dye tests.

In other cases the intake is less pronounced in central supply veins and occurs more uniformly and less dramatically across the whole width of the floret. The result is the initial extra development of the outer cell layer relative to the inner cell layer.

Thus we see first for purposes of cell expansion the activation of materials already in the cell, then further development due to the intake of sap-borne supplies of growth materials. But how does this affect floret and bloom form?

The outer cell layer differs in its composition relative to the inner layer and reacts differently during vacuolation. The evidence suggests that the cells of the outer cell layer contain more "growth materials" than those of the inner cell layer in the pre-vacuolate state, that is before the florets begin to unfold. This appears to apply particularly to incurves. Similarly, central tissues appear to contain proportionately more growth materials than tissues nearer to the margins of the floret. Consequently, when vacuolation is first triggered, and floret expansion is due almost entirely to the utilisation of materials already in its cells, the tissues of the outer cell layer will expand more than those of the inner cell layer, and central tissues will lengthen more than marginals, to induce the floret to develop at first in incurving form. The incurving form can be further intensified as supplies begin to enter the stronger central veins to further enlarge the more central tissues in their vicinity.

So we have the early stages of floret expansion due to the activation of materials already in the cells, with florets tending to develop in incurving form. Then, in some cases there is initial and relatively strong intake by the more central supply veins followed by steadier intake by other supply veins – or there may be a steady more uniform overall intake. In each case there is a tendency for the floret to expand somewhat uniformly over its whole area, though in incurving form, and in cases where the floret remains incurving this virtually uniform development continues throughout what is referred to as the "Grand Period of Growth" of the floret, that is until the development of the floret comes to an end.

But, as we have seen, the cells of the inner cell layer are composed differently from those of the outer cell layer. While in the pre-vacuolate stage they may have contained less sugars than those of the outer cell layer they appear to contain even less protein which makes them less respirative and more receptive and expansive to any growth materials now supplied directly from the leaves and roots.

Cells of the inner cell layer are more responsive to materials supplied by leaves and roots during vacuolation, for they are more able to make use of them for vacuolative purposes, and the same can be said of cells of more marginal tissues relative to those of central tissues. In fact, as vacuolation intensifies the cells of the inner cell layer are always endeavouring to expand to greater degree than those of the outer cell layer. In some cases the marginal tissues and floret tips of incurving florets can be seen to be endeavouring to roll over into the reflexing form, but reflexing is prevented by the extra length of more central tissues relative to marginals, keeping the floret bowed in incurving form.

Figure 18.2
A Floret Changing from Incurving to Reflexing

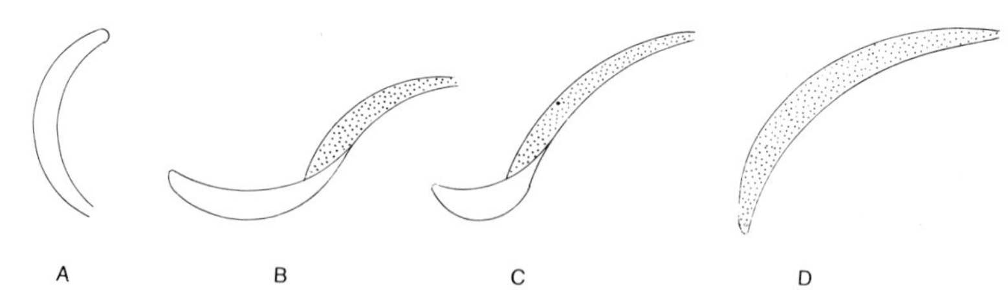

A=Floret at first incurving with outer cell layer more extensive than inner cell layer, and central tissues longer than marginals

B=Vacuolative impetus spreading from floret stub toward the tip to extend marginal tissues and promote reflexing

C=Floret reflexing progressively toward the tip

D=Floret now fully reflexed

Depending on the pre-vacuolative composition of its cells and on the nature of subsequent external supplies, a floret may continue in incurving form, enlarging steadily and relatively uniformly to the end of its grand period of growth, it may reflex relatively quickly and then continue its development in reflexing form, or it may remain basically incurving, but with a steady spread of extra vacuolative impetus from the stub of the floret toward the tip.

There appear to be two types of growth impetus in the floret, the basic relatively uniform development of the entire floret, which continues steadily through the grand period of growth, and a secondary wave of impetus, vigorous or weak, rapid or slow, which spreads from the stub of the floret toward the tip as intake by the veins increases, saturating the expansive capacity of successive rows of cells as it proceeds. This latter secondary impetus operates across the whole width of the floret, and logically it would have more effect on the more responsive marginal tissues and inner (upper) cells than on less responsive central tissues and outer (lower) cells; this results in the extra lengthening of marginal tissues and the extra swelling of the inner cells in the areas to which it has penetrated. As marginal tissues in a particular sector of the floret lengthen to equal those in the centre so the extra expansive capacity of the inner cell layer bows the floret both longitudinally and laterally into reflexing form. The cells nearest to the stub seem to commandeer supplies up to the point of their saturation before allowing them to pass through to rows of cells nearer to the tip. Thus a floret can reflex progressively from the stub toward the tip as the secondary sap-borne growth impulse travels quickly or more gradually along the floret.

In some cases this progressive reflexing – which can be looked upon as a form of extra floret development – will eventually reach to the tip to give a fully reflexing floret, but in other cases the grand period of growth will terminate before the reflexing impulse has reached the tip and the floret will be left as a reflex with an incurving tip.

This secondary impulse can in fact be *shown* to proceed longitudinally from the stub toward the tip, for the severing of marginal tissues on one side of the floret prevents the spread of reflexing on that side, while reflexing proceeds toward the tip on the unslit side. The marking of developing florets further indicates that expansion is greatest in the newly reflexing area and minimal in the incurving sectors nearer to the tip not yet reached by the secondary impetus.

The fact that variables tend to reflex more under low temperatures and that this is accompanied by improved anthocyanin colouration suggests a common factor, and we know that low temperature increases sugar concentrations, which in turn increases anthocyanin synthesis. It is therefore logical to assume that sugar is in fact an important agent of vacuolation, and that where it occurs in concentration reflexing is more likely, especially where accompanied during bloom development by a full supply of activating nutrients and associated hormones.

Practically, extra nutrition in the pre-bud and/or bud periods produces florets which tend to resist the change to reflexing; buds developing in long days tend to produce blooms which are more inclined to be incurving, and the same applies where plants are growing freely in rich soil; reduced cropping has been known to produce incurving blooms, as opposed to reflexing on a heavier crop; large pots of open compost favour incurving, and small pots and solid compost favour reflexing; high temperatures promote incurving, while low temperatures incline to reflexing.

Freshness

The ability of blooms to remain crisply fresh to the point of maturity varies with the variety. Some are "hard in petal" and durable, others tend to "tire" at the base before they are fully developed.

Problems are more likely to arise with large blooms which take a long time to open, and where feeding has been relatively heavy, especially with nitrogen, which makes for floret cells with thin walls. Smaller blooms on a less generous diet will have more substantial cell walls and are less likely to suffer "tiredness".

Once mature florets lose their turgidity there is a possibility that they will not recover, and therefore we must ensure that plants are never allowed to flag during the flowering period. For this reason a weak root system can be a primary cause of basal tiredness, especially under full sunshine and high temperatures. It follows that light shading will help to preserve blooms, and that open soils and composts which encourage root activity will benefit varieties with inherently weak root systems. Among the best and freshest blooms we have ever seen of a popular large incurve which normally tended to tire at the base were those grown by ring culture technique with roots running down into an open aggregate beneath bottomless whalehide pots.

Pinking

"Pinking" is the term applied to pink or red colouration developing on lower, older florets, most usually associated with whites and yellows, since it is more easily seen on them, though it is not confined to them.

It occurs under low temperatures, more especially where light is strong by day, which suggests sugar accumulation under conditions of low respiration and the consequent development of anthocyanin pigments.

The answer is quite simply to prevent temperatures falling too low during the flowering period. If temperature levels are kept at 50°F or above your chrysanthemums will not suffer "pinking". With lates flowering in the greenhouse the answer is to provide the necessary warmth, but with earlies in the garden, such temperature control is impossible. Fortunately, the problem mainly concerns whites and yellows, which can be bagged without colour loss, and if double bagging is resorted to (see p. 108) then the defect can be prevented. Double bagging appears to provide extra insulation against excessive drops in temperature.

Damping

"Damping" refers to the rotting of florets, which can be caused by conditions within the plant or external factors. Some varieties are prone to damping, others are "hard in petal" and relatively resistant.

Varieties which damp readily have thin cell walls and where these are made even thinner by cultural techniques or subjected to excessive inner pressures they fracture and release their contents, with resultant "damping".

Cell walls contain cellulose, derived from sugars made by the leaves, and where feeding has been excessive sugar concentrations will be reduced (see p. 93) and the materials from which the cell walls are made will be in limited supply. Furthermore, where nitrogen is in excess cell walls become more "elastic" and more subject to extension with the result that they can become thinner and rupture under the effects of osmotic pressure, in the same way that a balloon will burst if over-inflated.

External problems are mainly concerned with invasion by spores of fungi, in particular those of *Botrytis cinera* and *Itersonilia perplexans* (Petal Spot). Spores of such fungi need humid conditions for their germination, and when conditions are suitable they can cause damage in only a few hours. One night of excess humidity is certainly sufficient to cause widespread damage (see p. 114).

The answers are clearcut:

(a) Choose varieties not susceptible to damping;

(b) Do not overfeed, especially where a variety is known to be "soft in petal";

(c) Avoid sudden upsurges of moisture within the plant due to heavy watering, especially late in the day;

(d) Keep the atmosphere on the dry side during flowering, by providing sufficient heat in the greenhouse to keep the temperature 10°F above the outside level whenever the atmosphere is humid.

Foliage

Leaves are necessary to the existence and development of the plant and its blooms, but they are also desirable as the decorative backcloth to the blooms, more especially when they are cut and arranged in vases and bowls. It is therefore desirable that foliage is kept in good condition, and free of pests and diseases.

Leaves will be produced in attractive condition where nutrition is adequate but not excessive, and pests and diseases will be kept in check by routine sprays. But foliage will be made even more attractive where it is sprayed with a white oil preparation – usually in the form of a combined insecticide/fungicide – a week to ten days before blooms are cut. We can spend a whole twelve months producing just one crop of quality blooms and we should do everything we can to support them with quality foliage. The best chrysanthemums are indeed jewels of the horticultural world, and they deserve appropriate presentation.

APPENDIX I

Conversion Table

Linear measurements have been given in inches, feet and yards; measurements of volume in teaspoons, dessertspoons, tablespoons, pints and gallons; weights in ounces, pounds and hundredweights; temperature in degrees Fahrenheit. For practical purposes the following *approximate* conversions will suffice where metric measurements and the Celsius (centigrade) thermometer are in use.

1 inch = 2.5 centimetres
1 foot = 30 centimetres
1 yard = 1 metre

1 teaspoon = 5 millilitres
1 dessertspoon = 10 millilitres
1 tablespoon = 20 millilitres
1 pint = 0.6 litres
1 gallon = 4.5 litres

1 ounce = 28 grams
1 pound = 0.45 kilograms
1 hundredweight = 51 kilograms

Freezing point of water = 32°F (0°C)
Freezing point of chrysanthemum sap = 28.5°F (–2°C)
35°F = 2°C (approx.)
40°F = 4°C
50°F = 10°C
60°F = 15°C

APPENDIX II

Society Addresses

The following addresses may be of interest to those desiring further participation in chrysanthemum activities or seeking membership of an appropriate Society.

Great Britain

National Chrysanthemum Society
H.B. Locke, 2 Lucas House, Craven Road, Rugby, Warwickshire.

Australia

Chrysanthemum Society of Australia
Alan Littler, 20 Sunhill Avenue, Ringwood 3134, Victoria, Australia.

Royal Horticultural Society of Victoria
Mrs. N. Morley, Box 5000Y, Melbourne, Victoria, Australia.

Chrysanthemum Society of New South Wales
Bruce Skeen, 295 Blacktown Road, Blacktown N.S.W. 2148, Australia.

Canada

Canadian Chrysanthemum and Dahlia Society
G.H. Lawrence, 83 Araman Drive, Agincourt, Ont. M1T 2P7, Canada.

Point Grey Amateur Chrysanthemum Association
P. Baggaley, 3341 West 34th Ave., Vancouver V6N 2H1, Canada.

Victoria and District Chrysanthemum Society
Miss E.M. Henley, 2407 Esteran Ave., Victoria B.C., Canada, V8R 2S4.

Victoria Horticultural Society
Mrs. E. Whitlock, P.O. Box 5081, Postal Station B, Victoria B.C., Canada, V8R 6N3.

France

Societe Nationale D'Horticulture De France
84 Rue De Grenelle, Paris (VII), France.

Japan

Japan Chrysanthemum Society
Hirakata Park, Hirakata City, Osaka, Japan.

New Zealand

National Chrysanthemum Society of New Zealand
P.I. Strickland, 100A Hillcrest Road, Raumati Beach, Wellington, New Zealand.

M. Hollows, P.O. Box 767, Palmerston North, New Zealand.

South Africa

E. Arendse, 18 Juffernbruch Street, Idas Valley, Stellenbosch, South Africa.

United States

Chrysanthemum Society, Inc., U.S.A.
Joseph E. Millett, 4 Evergreen Court, Walnut Creek, California 94595.

Robert L. LeTourneau, 606 Sonoma Street, Richmond, California 94805.

The following organisations specialise in supplying chrysanthemums:

Great Britain

Riley's, Alfreton Nurseries, Woolley Moor, Derby.

Frank Rowe, Rylands Nurseries, Wellington, Somerset.

H. Walker, Oakfield Nurseries, Aldford Road, Huntington, Chester, Cheshire.

N. Walker, Belvedere Nurseries, Chapel Road, Hesketh Bank, Near Preston, Lancs.

H. Woolman Ltd., Grange Road, Dorridge, Solihull, Birmingham.

Alan Wren, Beechview Nursery, Avey Lane, Waltham Abbey, Essex.

Japan

Yoshihiko Yamate, Kanemaru, Shinichi-cho, Ashina-District, Hiroshima-pref., Japan.

New Zealand

Leo Clark, 6 Bowenvale Avenue, Christchurch 2, New Zealand.

United States

Huff's Garden Mums, 710 Juanitta, Box 187, Burlington, Kansas 66839.

King's Chrysanthemums, PO Box 368, Clements, California 95227.

May's Mums, 2024 Staunton Avenue, N.W., Roanoke, Va. 24017.

Sunnyslope Gardens, 8638 Huntingdon Drive, San Gabriel, CA 91775.

In the event of difficulty of supply it is suggested that advice be sought from the officials of Societies listed for the various countries.

Index

aeration: in soils and composts 47-50, 54, 56, 58, 83; in the plant 47
AM (Award of Merit) 22
anemones: bloom qualities 119; classifications 19-20
aphids 34-5, 64, 86, 108, 113, 135
aspermy virus 23, 137

bagging, blooms of earlies 107
basal growths, trimming 27-8, 88, 113-14
bedding earlies 64, 67
bird damage 79, 85
blind shoots 136
bloom: colour 105, 137, 150-4; dressing 121-2, 124; feeding 108-10, 113, 149; form 137, 154-9; freshness 159-60; keeping 127; pinking 108, 137, 160; qualities 118-19; size 26, 69-70, 91-102 *passim*, 147-50; tiredness 137
blooms flagging 128
blooms malformed 137
bonsai 21; cultivation 133-4
borders, plants in 80
botrytis cinerea 115, 161
bowls and baskets, exhibiting 120
break bud 68-9
bud: feeding 99-100; initiation 96-7; movement in 98-100; sequence 68-9
buds damaged 136
buds rotting 136
buying plants 22-3, 35-6

calcium 50, 52
calyx break 102, 148
capsid bug 86, 103, 135
cascades: classification 20; cultivation 130
caterpillars 86, 108, 113, 135, 137
cell division 98-9, 147
cell vacuolation 98, 147-8, 157
chalk 48, 51-4
charms: classification 20; cultivation 129
Christmas flowering 134
classification system 18-21
coarse blooms 137
colour groups 21
colour in blooms 102, 105, 114, 150-4
composts: condition when potting 60; for final pots 81; for first pots 60; for propagation 39; for second pots 66; for stools 29; ideal mixture 50; physical condition 46-50
conditions of growth 94-5, 147
conversion tables 162
countdown 87, 99
covering earlies 105-6
cut blooms for decoration 127-8
cuttings: ideal 37; rooting condition 38; rooting needs 38-9; when to insert 38-9

daily rounds 86
daisy eye 123, 137
damping of blooms 114-15, 137, 160-1
damping of stools growths 34
daylength and bloom form 137, 159
daylength and bud development 71
deshooting and disbudding 88, 96
dry weight 92-3; theory 26
dwarf pot plants, cultivation 132

earlies: bloom protection 104-8; flowering of 104-10; planting 78-80; plot preparation 55-9; rooting dates 39
early-flowering classifications 20-1
early-flowering sprays: classification 21; cultivation 132
earwigs 86, 102, 108, 113, 137
eelworm 24, 88, 135
elliptical bloom centres 137
espaliers, cultivation 130-1
exhibiting 117-26; NCS Rules 17-18; NCS Points System 120-1

FCC (First Class Certificate) 23
feeding 91-5, 99-100, 102; balanced 91; basic patterns 92-4; bloom 108-10, 113; cessation of 102;

earlies 91, 100; in bud 99-100; lates 91-5, 99-100; stools 33-4; varietal adjustments 101
final potting 81-5
first crown buds 68-9
floret: construction 98-9, 108, 147, 151; count 75, 96; development 147, 154-9; initiation 96-7; veinal supply 151, 156-7
foliage: conditioning sprays 110; discoloured 135; distorted in tips 136; mottled 135; quality of 161; reddened 135; speckled 135; tunnelled 135; withering 135; yellowing 135
frame ventilation 35, 62
froghoppers 103
fumigation 111, 113

greenhouse: fumigation 111, 113; heating 32, 42, 115-16; insulation 31; preparation for flowering 111; shading 43, 111; ventilation 31-2, 42, 112, 114-16
growth retardents 43, 95-6

hardening 62-4
heating methods 32-3, 115-16
hormones 147, 149
housing lates 111-12
humidity during flowering 114-15
humus 56-7

imported plants 64
incurved: bloom qualities 118-19; classifications 18, 20
intermediate: bloom qualities 119; classifications 19-20
iron 52
itersonilia perplexans 161

Jeyes Fluid 28-9, 65, 102, 111
John Innes base fertilisers 53-4
John Innes composts 29, 39, 48-55, 60, 65, 81

large exhibition: bloom qualities 118; classification 18; rooting dates 38
large October-flowering classification 20
late-flowering: classifications 18-20; rooting dates 38
late-flowering sprays: classification 19; cultivation 132-3; rooting dates 39
laterals: countdown 87, 99; leaf count and length 26, 69; long V development 46, 69, 91, 147
lates: final potting 81-4, pot sizes 82; flowering 111-16; housing 111
leaf count, importance of 69
leaf miner 34, 64, 87, 135
leaf-shine sprays 110
leafy gall 24, 135
leaves as barometers 95
leaves, the role of 92-5
light and bloom colour 105, 152-3
lime 51-2, 58
loam stacking 48-9

magnesium 52
manuring 57-8
measurement conversions 162
medium exhibition: bloom qualities 118; classification 18; rooting dates 38
mildew 87, 110, 113, 136
mulching 100-1

natural breaks 74
natural development 25, 68-9
nitrogen 51, 92, 149
nutrition: and bloom form 155-9; and cell development 99-100, 108-9, 147-9; and the soil 57-8; balanced 53; essential elements 51-3

October flowering: classifications 20; rooting dates 38-9
ordering plants 35-6
overall aim 25-6
overhead covers 105-7

PC (Preliminary Commendation) 22
peat 49
pests in frames 34, 64
petal spot 161
pH 48-52 *passim*; and the soil 58
phosphorus 51, 92
photosynthesis 92-3
pigments: anthocyanin 151-4; anthoxanthin 151-2; carotenoids 151-3; colour loss 105, 153
pillars, cultivation of 130
pinking, bloom 108, 137, 160
planting out earlies 78-80
plot preparation for earlies 55-8, 78
pompons: classifications 19-21; qualities 119
pot sizes, finals 82
potassium 51, 92
potting on 65-7
potting up 60-1
propagation: in greenhouse 37-43; in frames 43-45

quills classification 19

Index

ray blight 113, 136
reflexed: bloom qualities 119; classifications 18, 20
respiration 93, 150, 155
ripeness of growth 101
rooting cuttings: dates 38-9; greenhouse temperature 42; greenhouse ventilation 42; ideal method 40-1; in frames 43; in greenhouse 37-43; rooting mediums 39; soil temperature 38-40; watering 42; when to root 38-9
roots, oxygen needs 47
run-by 76

sand for composts 49
second crown buds 68-9
Sequestrene 53
shading: earlies in bloom 105; lates in bloom 111; rooting cuttings 43
singles: bloom qualities 119; classifications 19-21; rooting dates 38
size in the bloom 26, 69-70, 91-102 *passim*, 147-50
slugs 35, 43, 64, 110, 135
soil: aeration 47; ideal blend 50; physical condition 46-50, 55-8; preparation 55-9; types 47-8, 55-6
soilless composts 54
specimen plants: cultivation 131; exhibiting 119
spiders classification 19
spoons classification 19
spraying routine 87
sprays: bloom qualities 119; classifications 19-21; cultivation 132-3; exhibiting 119
staging exhibits 121-2
standard plants, cultivation 130-1
standing ground for lates 84-5
stem cuttings 27
stems: as barometers 101; bent 136; splitting 136
sterilisation of loam 54
sterilisation of soils 54
stock selection 23-5, 61, 67, 110, 116
stools: bedding materials 29; earlies, lifting and boxing 28; in frames 34-5; feeding 34; growths numbers 27; growths timing 28; pests 53; temperatures 31-2; watering 33; wintering 27-35
stopping 68-74; condition 71; earlies 70; lates 71; reasons for 68
stunt virus 23
sugars: and bloom colour 152; and bloom form 155-7; and cell development 99, 147-50

temperature: and bloom colour 153-4; and bloom form 155; and bud initiation 70; and cell development 150; conversions 162; for bud development 102; for flower development 114-15; for propagation 39-40, 42; for wintering stools 31
terminal buds 68-9
timing 74-6; bud to colour 76; colour to full bloom 76; cuttings to stop 74; stop to bud 75-6
tomato aspermy virus 23
top dressings 100
tortrix moth 86, 135
trace elements 53
troubles and cures 135-7
two-leaf stop 74

varieties, choosing 22-3
vaseline beneath buds 102-3
ventilation: during propagation 42; of frames 35, 62; of lates during flowering 112, 114-16; of wintering stools 31-2
verticillium wilt 24, 88, 135
virus B 23
virus disease 23, 137

water and vacuolation 149
watering: after final potting 84; cuttings 42; earlies in flower 108; earlies in growth 86, 90; lates in flower 111-13; lates in growth 86, 90; principles 63; stools 33
weekly rounds 86
white rust 87